COME AND SEE

The Beguiling Story of the Tyneside Cinema

by Michael Chaplin

For my Dad, who first took me to the pictures

Published by New Writing North in conjunction with Tyneside Cinema
Holy Jesus Hospital
City Road
Newcastle upon Tyne
NE1 2AS
Tel: +44 (0) 191 233 3850
www.newwritingnorth.com

ISBN 978-0-9566551-1-0

Design by David McClure
Tel: +44 (0) 7946 642 161
www.velcrobelly.co.uk

Printed by Martins the Printers
Sea View Works
Spittal
Berwick-upon-Tweed
Northumberland
TD15 1RS
Tel: +44 (0) 1289 306 006
www.martins-the-printers.co.uk

Typeset in Garamond Premier Pro and Schadow Black Condensed

Tyneside Cinema is a company limited by guarantee registered in England & Wales: 502 592
Tyneside Cinema is a registered charity in England & Wales: 11 13 101
VAT registration: 178 1689 18

Tyneside Cinema
10 Pilgrim Street
Newcastle upon Tyne
NE1 6QG
Tel: +44 (0) 845 217 9909
Email: comeandsee@tynesidecinema.co.uk
www.tynesidecinema.co.uk

Contents

'If you don't like, don't listen, but I can tell you a story...'

From the journal of Dixon Scott, founding father and cinema pioneer, found and rescued from a skip outside Tyneside Cinema, 1983

Introduction

One evening in the mid Nineties, a young Procter and Gamble executive called Simon Elliott took his heavily-pregnant wife Julie to the Tyneside Cinema. The film was *Ed Wood*, Tim Burton's entertaining biopic of the maker of hilariously bad horror movies. At one point during the film, a character gave a bloodcurdling shriek, and Julie's unborn baby responded by swivelling in the womb. This was the last time the parents-to-be visited the cinema before Phoebe Elliott was born, but it seems to have been a momentous event for all concerned. Phoebe has grown up loving the cinema (and has held more than one birthday party there), while the affection her mother and father share for the Tyneside has its roots in their memory of the night it entered the unfolding history of their family.

While I was researching this book, just about everyone I met seemed to have a Tyneside story – and their own particular and personal relationship with it, which deepens with every passing year.

I suppose the same is true for me.

I have no memory of going to the News Theatre that occupied the building before it, but I know I first went to the Tyneside in 1968, the year it opened, to see an old French movie called *La Kermesse Héroïque*. I loved it. I was also hooked by the idea of old French movies, and the place where I sat in the darkness watching it.

Before we left Newcastle to go to university, my then-girlfriend and now-wife Susan and I went to the Tyneside a lot. We saw *2001: A Space Odyssey* there – or maybe that was with my friend Charlie? – and made many other discoveries, of films and film-makers, including François Truffaut, a perennial favourite. Over the years that followed, the place played a key role in developing not only my cinematic education, but also in fuelling the urge to become a storyteller myself. Now all these years later, the Tyneside Cinema remains, alongside Live Theatre, my cultural destination of choice in Newcastle, not just for what it shows, but also for what it is, and how all of that connects to my past. I just love the place.

Little wonder then that I jumped at the chance to tell its story. But a few months ago not even I could have imagined quite how rich that story really was. As a consequence the project – and the book that's emerged from it – has grown.

What follows is not solely a history of a building or a cultural organisation, but hopefully a richer story. This is partly because of the many remarkable people who've been associated with the cinema in its various guises since it opened. Perhaps the daddy of them all is Dixon Scott Senior, who deserves his own place in cinema history – and not merely because he was the great-uncle of the film-making brothers Ridley and Tony Scott.

The more I discovered about the life and career of the cinema's remarkable founding father, who opened his first cinema in Jarrow in 1908, exactly 100 years before his last cinema in Pilgrim Street reopened after extensive renovation, the more I began to see that in a way this book could be a history of cinema itself, reflected through the life of one picture house in a corner of England, the experiences of the people who ran it and the other people who sat in its red seats.

Finally, in the stories of all of these individuals – some of whose considerable lives are described in separate biographical panels scattered throughout the book – I thought it might be possible to sketch the beginnings of a social history of that place over the last century.

That, anyway, has been my ambition – to create a narrative out of some compelling human stories. Just like a good film, in fact.

I hope you enjoy this beguiling tale.

Michael Chaplin
Newcastle upon Tyne
March 2011

Opposite page:
The Cowardly Lion and
percussive pal scar the psyches
of Newcastle's children in the
hope of drumming up trade.

1 | 'It's like the Blair Witch Project down there...'

It's 9.30am on a sunny Thursday morning in late August 2010, the shadow of the Northern Counties Club in Hood Street etched high on the wall of the Tyneside Cinema. In High Friar Lane, the pavement outside the Intermezzo coffee bar is being swept as it opens for business, but the doors of the cinema next door remain locked. Despite that, the place is already humming inside.

In the foyer, supervisor Rebecca Innes is waking up her box office to a new day – switching lights and computers on, changing times for the day's screenings, signing on the police radio in case of trouble (the lane attracts the 'occasional scallywag'), and checking emails from customers.

In his office, chief executive Mark Dobson is sipping a coffee as finance manager Martin Horrocks shows him a spreadsheet tracking all of the cinema's sales and ticket yields on a day by day basis.

In the bar, venue manager Leigh Venus is looking for a place to store his popcorn to make way for a new line in glasses, of the optical kind – the cinema is shortly installing 3D. In the Coffee Rooms downstairs – a Tyneside institution inside an institution – proprietor John Oswell is making last-minute checks on the day's menu before the doors open. Thursday is always a busy day.

And as the Northern Goldsmiths clock strikes ten, I start work on my Tyneside project, recording the story of this building and all who've sailed in her.

I want to start by touring the cinema and getting a feel for it. I've been here countless times since my family came to Newcastle in the late Fifties, but I want to see the bits the public never see – the dark spaces and quiet corners that maybe tell a different kind of story.

Programme manager Jonny Tull, who's worked here since 1994, is my guide. We stand in the foyer, our feet on the gleamingly-restored mosaic floor, assembled in 1936 by Italian craftsmen as the cinema's founder, Dixon Scott Senior, looked on in pride, then covered over 40 years later with cheap grey bathroom tiles in a forlorn attempt to look 'modern'.

We descend into the stalls of Scott's original News Theatre, now the Classic, and I gaze again at its traditional red curtain and the frame of its proscenium arch, a reference to the music halls where Scott opened his first cinemas in the 1900s. To its side is a hook on the wall, on which used to hang a clock to remind some News Theatre customers that their bus would soon be leaving Worswick Street bus station down the road.

As we return to the box office, Rebecca Innes is talking to a regular customer about films she may like to see, just as another lady arrives for breakfast in the Coffee Rooms, as she does like clockwork every day.

Jonny leads me down some steep steps into the basement. 'It's like the *Blair Witch Project* down here,' he says. We turn up all manner of detritus from the past: two ancient safes, presumably empty; a disco mirror-ball, minus some of its glitter (the remains, I later discover, of a Eurovision Song Contest party of years before); a metal screen from the circle; a solitary toilet and, to complete the sanitary theme, some bottles of Saniloo Germ-Killing Powder.

Down here amid the debris and the rumble of Metro trains a hundred feet down, Charlie Picken, the cinema's manager in the early 70s, had his office until Dixon Scott Junior took pity on him and let him have an office that didn't have a view of the boiler room.

Upstairs, house manager Samantha Simpson is walking around the building to make sure it's ready for the public, ensuring fire exits are clear and turning on the cinema heritage displays on the first and second floors. Finance manager Martin Horrocks is making his usual analysis of the previous day's box office returns and discovers that the week's target for admissions have been hit with a day to spare – and without a blockbuster in sight, bar one preview screening of *Scott Pilgrim vs. The World*. The star of the week is *The Illusionist*, the Tati-inspired animation set in Edinburgh, but everything else has done quite well too, except for the Stallone-and-other-aging-stars action epic *The Expendables*, which has, says Martin, 'bombed horribly'.

Before the first screening of the day in the Classic at 11.30am – the daily newsreel archive film, today featuring an original account of the independence celebrations in India and Pakistan in August 1947, as well as a local Scout Jamboree – Jonny and I explore the Circle, walking between brown leather armchairs and sofas installed by Italian craftsmen of a later era, who in 2008, like The Devil, wore Prada.

Jonny opens a door into a long, narrow space on two levels. He calls it 'the secret room', as it was rediscovered around 2003 after being blocked off for many years. When workmen broke in, they discovered, rather eerily, that the light had been left on. It was here, 70 years ago, that cinema usherettes like Molly Alexander would have their tea breaks, stockinged feet on stools, brewing up on a little gas ring, the voices of the newsreel commentators braying on the other side of an old curtain.

The room is used now for storing paper cups and old posters, among them *The Dark Knight* and Terence Davies' evocation of post-war Liverpool, *Time and the City*.

Front of house assistant Alison Hayes opens up the Classic to the first paying customers of the day, for the 12.30pm screening of *The Illusionist*.

In the projection box at the back of the Classic Circle, projectionist Ray Reed, who started his apprenticeship here as a 16-year-old a few weeks after England's World Cup triumph of 1966, presses the button to start the French animation. This is transmitted digitally from a hard drive – only the adverts are screened in the traditional way, from the so-called 'cake-stand' arrangement of spools to a Kinoton projector – but seeing Ray peering through a tiny glass window at the distant screen, one is inevitably reminded of *Cinema Paradiso*. Soon Ray will be climbing the spiral staircase connecting this box to the projection boxes for the Roxy and the Electra, where the gripping Argentine thriller *The Secret in Their Eyes* will flicker into life. No wonder Ray looks trim – he says he's 'up and down them stairs like the whore's drawers'.

In the Coffee Rooms early luncheon is being served. Today's specials are black pudding with roasted root vegetables and scampi and chips, but perennial favourites like poached eggs on toast and egg and chips are doing well. Five tables are crowded with groups John Oswell describes as 'ladies who lunch' – Thursdays and Fridays are particularly popular – and they're having a laugh. The room hums with conversation. Mark Dobson is having fish and chips with local film-maker Richard Fenwick and mentions an idea of projects manager Holli McGuire to commission a new musical score to three pieces of historic shipbuilding film from the BFI National Archive. Richard is interested in the idea of working on the reinterpretation of the films and goes off to the BFI Mediatheque at the Discovery Museum to check out the film, *Tyneside*, which charts the building of a luxury liner at Swans in 1938.

Details of the Tyneside Cinema's unique blend of art deco and Persian design.

Photos © Sally Ann Norman (first left) and Allan Mushen

In the box office, Rebecca is signing for a delivery of reels of film and tidying the lost property cupboard; house manager Samantha is cashing up from the night before, then off to the bank to deposit the takings and collect some change before doing a stint as relief usher in the Classic circle; Martin is redrafting the Articles of Association for the Cinema in a new age and Leigh has finally found a place to put his popcorn.

Jonny leads me to the room next to the Coffee Rooms on the second floor: the Digital Lounge, a cool interior with black walls and a large screen. It was very different 70 years ago. Then it was the Tyne Room, a private space conceived by Dixon Scott Senior, like the Smoke Room nearby, for the use of businessmen in the morning and their wives in the afternoon. He commissioned local artist Bessie Carr to decorate its walls with a mural of local scenes, among them Bamburgh Castle, Seaton Sluice, Newcastle's bridges, and slightly more surprisingly, Prudhoe. But Scott was fond of Prudhoe – he had a picture house there called the Electric. Bessie also decorated the Coffee Rooms with a mural depicting *The Canterbury Tales*, though it's unclear if the bawdy story of the Wife of Bath was included – given Scott's distaste for anything that smacked of smut, possibly not. Water damage from a fire in the then Cinema 2 upstairs (now the Roxy) in 1975 destroyed both murals.

We then move east towards the front of the building, though a door into the wood-panelled Newe House, where the Tyneside's 50-strong staff is based. Here Holli McGuire is preparing an application to the Arts Council for specially-commissioned music for the shipbuilding films project and Jonny makes final plans for the cinema's programme in late September, including the films *Made in Dagenham*, *Wall Street 2* and *A Town Called Panic*. Mark Dobson gets an invite from Radio 5 to go on the Mark Kermode and Simon Mayo show when the station transmits from Newcastle in September and then heads off home to see his son, Finlay, who's recovering from chickenpox.

I explore the rooms on this floor and above. They've all performed numerous functions over the last 73 years: the office that belonged to the Dixon Scotts is now a staffroom, with giant fridge and broadband; the Headspace Room – for individual contemplation and group brainstorming – was once Newcastle's American Consulate, with Stars and Stripes fluttering from a pole outside its window; the Figgis Room was once the Newcastle Buddhist Centre and a religious shrine, rather appropriate given that the cinema stands on the site of a medieval Franciscan priory, hence the origin of the name of High Friar Lane below.

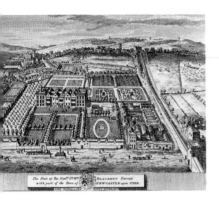

Above: Anderson Place, The Seat of the Honourable Sir Wm Blackett, Baronet, with Pilgrim Street on right. Future Tyneside Cinema in gardens in north east corner of the Blackett estate.

In the 17th century the land stood at the north east corner of a substantial property belonging to Newcastle merchant William Blackett. Just inside the northern city walls, Anderson Place was surrounded by orchards and the extravagantly pretty Nuns Gardens, around which Blackett would walk every morning.

There are many stories to be told about the Tyneside Cinema, the land it stands upon and the people associated with both, and here is the first, as recorded by a Victorian hagiographer of Blackett, 200 years after his death. It reads like a plotline in a 1930s Hollywood biopic...

'Soon after he commenced business, Sir William risked his all in a speculation in flax, and having freighted a large vessel with that article received the unpleasant intelligence that the flax fleet had been dispersed in a storm, and the vessels lost or captured by the enemy. He took his accustomed walk next morning, ruminating on his loss, and was aroused by the noise of a ship in the river. He jumped upon an adjoining hedge, hailed the vessel and found it to be his own, which had weathered the storm. He instantly rode in a short time to London and hastened to the exchange, found the merchants in great alarm about the loss of the flax fleet and the consequent high price of flax. On informing them that he dealt in that article and had a large quantity to dispose of, speculators soon flocked around him and he sold his cargo at a most extravagant price, and the produce of that adventure laid the foundation for one of the largest fortunes ever acquired in Newcastle. Sir William regarded with a kind of veneration the hedge from which he first perceived the vessel and made it the extent of his future morning walks.'

Back to the future.

Below: Tyneside Cinema's hugely popular knitting club, A Good Yarn.

In the third floor bar, manager Neil Watson is preparing for Free Film Night, one of many events in the bar, including the hugely popular Film Quiz and Knitting Club, run by venue manager Leigh Venus. This one is Neil's own baby: 'We show films in the bar, which I pushed for after I was hired. I'd noticed the projector in the bar and I was reminded of a little bar I visited in Edinburgh during the Fringe. They showed films twice daily, I watched *Jaws*, then *The Godfather*. Films in a bar? Genius!' Tonight's movie is *Abre los Ojos,* later remade as *Vanilla Sky*. Neil is looking forward to catching some of it – between serving cocktails. As it turned out, bar sales (with which the cinema wipes its face for providing these free screenings) were disappointing, less than half that for *Spinal Tap*.

As Jonny leaves me to finish his working day – the planning of a special event featuring the work of musician Steven Severin – I head back to the Coffee Rooms. It's more crowded than ever, and the usual eclectic mix of clientele: a young man is tweeting at the next table, an academic I know is reading an account of the Miners' Strike, a gay couple hold hands, an elderly man holds tickets for his family party for the early evening screening of *The Illusionist*. A young mother shares quiche and salad with her toddler daughter, then her partner arrives, obviously from work, and the tea is split three ways. Two elderly women are sucking milkshakes through straws and giggling. I can't restrain myself any longer – and succumb to a huge portion of apple pie and custard.

It's a busy evening at the Tyneside. *The Illusionist* and *The Secret in Their Eyes*, both building into sleeper hits, do good business and the bar is packed for a ravishing Spanish tale of love and plastic surgery. During the course of the day, almost 500 tickets are sold, but many more use the building, including those touring its heritage displays, watching the free movie and eating highly popular comfort food in the Coffee Rooms. On average, 300 people daily park themselves on the café's plush red chairs. In total, about 1,200 people visit the building every day.

As I scoop up the last of the custard, I ponder something Jonny had told me earlier. We were standing in the long corridor that runs east to west on the second floor of Newe House, where he has his office. It was there, late one night in the mid Nineties, that a member of staff came out of her office, glanced along the corridor and saw a strange figure standing looking at her from the other end. She asked if she could help, but the figure, who seemed to be wearing some sort of robe or cloak, didn't reply. And when she looked back, it had vanished.

Over the years other members of staff have heard unexplained voices in various parts of the labyrinthine building. Cleaners working one day in the old Cinema 2 saw shadowy figures on the stage and promptly scarpered, thoroughly spooked.

Then there's Charlie Picken's story. In the early 70s, the then cinema manager got a call from a rattled projectionist in Cinema 1 who told him that in mid-film, the projector had stopped running, the curtain came down and the house-lights up. He couldn't explain these events – separate switches controlled the functions. His unease increased when the sequence reversed: lights, curtain, film. There was no mechanical or electrical explanation for these and similar events in Cinema 2 later that day. So Charlie reached for a Ouija board, which indicated a 'presence'.

Above: The Exorcist pays a visit to Tyneside Cinema to promote 'The North East's Favourite Scary Film' halloween campaign in 2009.

Opposite page: The Scott family band, early 1890s. From left, 'handsome, arrogant Tot' on cello, Harry without instrument, Marie on violin, Eddie on viola, JR on violin, and Dixon on flute and piccolo.

These manifestations of the other-worldly once prompted Jonny Tull to call in a team of psychic investigators (Tyneside's own Ghostbusters) with a van-full of monitoring devices. I sense this was a bit of a lark on his part, though he reports gleefully that they did get excited at finding several 'cold spots'. I said he should send them round to my house in February.

But I do remember what Ridley Scott told me. Not the film director Ridley Scott but his younger cousin, the IT consultant from Hertfordshire. His father Dixon Scott Junior ran the News Theatre, on and off, from 1937 to 1968 and as a boy Ridley used to visit him there, on Saturdays and during school holidays. He was often left to his own devices and liked exploring the cinema's far corners – but not before the audiences started arriving at 10.30am. 'There is nothing quite so scary as an empty cinema – it used to really spook me,' he tells me down a crackly line.

As it happens, I've never really believed in things that go bump in the night, let alone in broad daylight. But I've come to believe that there is a sense in which the Tyneside is indeed haunted, but in a benign way – its ghosts are friendly spirits, who cherished the building and loved it with a passion, and laboured hard to build and improve it, keep it going against all odds, and in the process make Newcastle a better place in which to live. Many of these people are now dead – how I wish I could have had a natter with them all in the Coffee Rooms – but as someone else featured in this book said in another context, 'the song is over, but the chords go on vibrating'.

During the writing of this book, I heard lots of distant music, but perhaps the loudest, full of sounding brass, came from the cinema's founder, the remarkable Dixon Scott Senior...

I finally leave the Tyneside Cinema at six, mind spinning with ideas, characters, lost rooms and projectors that suddenly stopped turning.

In the box office, supervisor Rebecca Innes records the screening times for the week ahead on the Tyneside's telephone system and also heads for home, making her usual silent farewell.

Good night and God bless, Tyneside – until tomorrow.

2 | 'We'll go again to the Kino, where the films are fine-o...'

Above: Graphic designer and treasure-trover Rob Barnes.

One day in the mid-1980s, a young graphic designer called Rob Barnes passed a skip outside the Tyneside Cinema, where he worked at the time. The cinema was undergoing one of its periodic makeovers, but this time the people responsible had maybe gone too far with their titivating.

Later in this book Elaine Cusack describes finding a now-treasured sign to the Coffee Rooms in the same skip, and there are rumours of various living rooms in Jesmond and Heaton decorated with coloured window-panes and other pieces of art deco detailing from the cinema. A similar thing happened at Dixon Scott's other Newcastle cinema, the Haymarket, when it was demolished at about the same time, and one lucky passer-by rescued – and kept – some very impressive doors abandoned in *their* skip.

What Rob saw was less bulky, but no less interesting – some fine mahogany shelving, and a book, more correctly two, but one of them – a full record of the News Theatre's receipts over the years – was too badly damaged by water (probably the after-effects of a fire in the mid Seventies) to be worth keeping. But he did take home the other book – a brown leather and cloth ledger-style volume – and examined it carefully. He was much intrigued by what he read, and kindly loaned it back to the cinema, where I was able to study it in detail 25 years later.

I opened it with excitement because it seemed to offer an insight into the life and times – and innermost thoughts – of the man whose photo portrait hangs on the stairs of the cinema, its 'founding father' as the caption reads, Dixon Scott Senior. He is dressed immaculately, with Homburg hat, wing collar and bow-tie, gloves and cane, but more arresting is the bespectacled face – alert, intelligent, sensitive, slightly anxious. As you look at it, you're intrigued, and wonder: who exactly was Dixon Scott?

The book seems to promise an answer, for the journal is clearly his, dated 27 September 1932 on its page of contents, which include such sections as Fables; Poems; Vignettes; Books To Be Written (on cinema, democracy, 'one in Finnish setting and one in Turkish setting'); Some Old Russian Expressions; Metaphors; and 'Some Notes for Debate on Disarmament'. There is also a list of 'Xmas Cards Received 1936'. Here, it seems, was a businessman with an interesting intellectual hinterland.

Then, the first disappointment. Turn the pages and what you see, in blue ink and elegant hand, is shorthand, lots and lots of shorthand: Dixon Scott keeping the voyeur at bay.

Then, the first surprise. Tyneside Cinema chief executive Mark Dobson is as tantalised as I am and tracks down someone who can transcribe the fiendishly difficult Pitman New Era Shorthand. This was launched in 1922, but is now more or less extinct. Dave and Jill Stevens of Pitman Training Newcastle put him in touch with Judith Milne of Billericay in Essex, who agrees to tackle the book – and in time the text appears on my desk, albeit with significant gaps. Sadly, much of what Dixon Scott hurriedly wrote in his book is now too faded to read...

So to the second disappointment. It soon becomes clear that the journal wasn't written for anyone but Dixon Scott himself. It is in fact a *writer's* notebook, full of jottings to be expanded and developed later by the man holding the pen with the very fine point. As a result, it is elusive, elliptical, and rather maddening. Most of the scribblings relate to Scott's long and pioneering career in the cinema business on Tyneside, but there's no clear narrative to follow.

There are instead glimpses of hidden riches: his projected novel is to be called *The White Spot*; a reference to an effigy of King George V being paraded across the street from Scott's cinema in Jarrow, on the day of the Coronation of 1910; a memory of 'The Ropery Banks, North Shields where I saw my first cine "movie pictures". Additional attraction. It was a short picture of a train journey, look through window, girl undressing, tunnel just at interesting part!'

But this is all texture. The story just isn't there. Pieces of Dixon Scott can be found in his journal, but it's impossible to join them up and construct the whole man.

There are further glimpses elsewhere, among the Tyneside's four boxes of archives, in the obituaries that followed his death in February 1939, two years after the opening of the News Theatre – a line of facts shunted together like freight cars.

After he left school he worked for a time with the Tyne Iron Shipbuilding Company.

While still in his teens he went to the Caucasus in Russia to work in the oilfields for two years.

Returning to England, he was connected to the Hexham and District Electric Supply Co. Ltd.

At various times he owned and ran picture halls in South and North Shields and Prudhoe, as well as Newcastle.

He was a prominent Freemason, a senior Past Master of Ridley Lodge, Newcastle; Past President of North Shields Literary and Debating Society, member of Newcastle's Pen and Palette Club and the Tynemouth Photographic Society.

He stood as a Conservative candidate for Tynemouth in the General Election of 1918, but was not elected.

And among the yellowing newspaper clippings, there's one quote summing up the man that catches the eye: 'His career was one of constant action and movement.' But sadly, depressingly, much of that career remains hidden, everything from how he built up his cinema empire to why he learnt shorthand. His life is in shadow.

Then out of the blue the sun comes out.

Dixon Scott had three sons, one of whom, his namesake, took over the business after his death. Dixon Junior had eight children from two marriages, two of whom died in childhood. I track down the other six, scattered from Cumbria to North Carolina, and they are all hugely helpful, but of course none of them knew their grandfather or can add much flesh to the bare bones of his life.

However, one of them, Anthea Guthrie, mentions a book in a drawer, written by her Great-Uncle Bob, Dixon's brother. It might be worth a look, she says. So I book a flight to Cardiff, and so find myself one day in the Vale of Glamorgan, sitting in a conservatory warmed by late summer sun and opening *A Family Named Scott (The Last and Least of It)*, by Bob Scott. The book, a collection of 131 immaculately typed sheets, was written in 1977 'in a dingy flat third floor back' a few minutes from Brighton's sea front, by the solitary – and by the sound of it, rather lonely – 81-year-old retired cinema manager. The whole story is there – and what a story, like the gold Dixon's brother William went looking for in South Africa's Gold Rush (which naturally, this being real life, he didn't find)...

To begin at the beginning...

Above: Robert Forster Octave Scott, Dixon's younger brother and eventual biographer, photographed in 1938 on being appointed manager of the Forum, Liverpool.

Opposite page: Dixon Scott, Tyneside Cinema's founding father.

Photo restoration by RWDP

A FAMILY NAMED SCOTT

Richard Scott — Margaret Bell

- John Richard (JR)
  - Edward (Eddie)
- Maria (Marie)
  - Thomas Bell
- William Forster
- Unnamed Twins (died at birth)
- Septimus
  - Henry Michael (Harry)
- Margaret Bell
  - Edith
  - Robert Forster Octave (Bob)

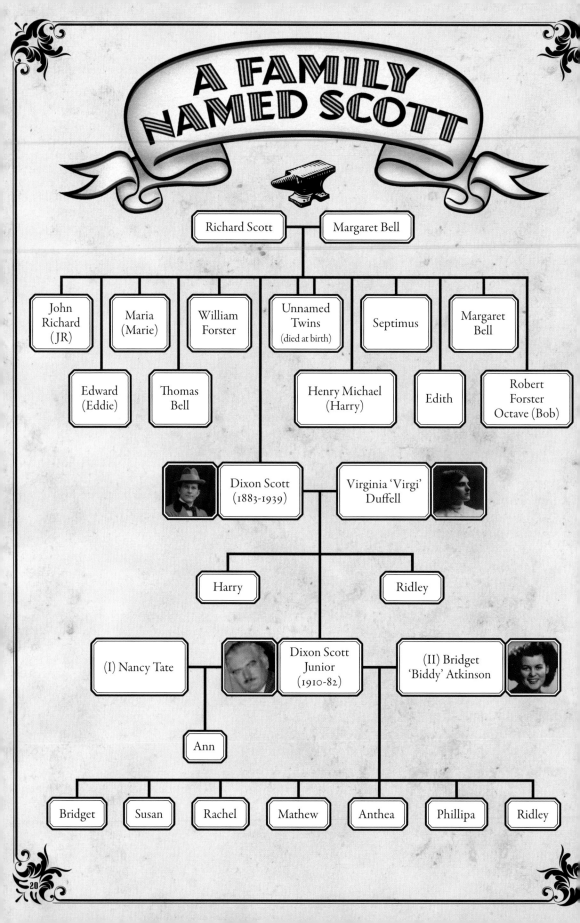

Dixon Scott (1883-1939) — Virginia 'Virgi' Duffell

- Harry
- Ridley

(I) Nancy Tate — Dixon Scott Junior (1910-82) — (II) Bridget 'Biddy' Atkinson

- Ann

- Bridget
- Susan
- Rachel
- Mathew
- Anthea
- Phillipa
- Ridley

Once upon a time in the second half of Queen Victoria's reign there was a blacksmith who lived in North Shields. His name is Richard Scott. He's proud of the fact that he's the seventh generation of blacksmiths in his family, who originally hail from Belford. It turns out he'll be the last. Bob Scott remembers his grandfather – he had, he says, 'a face of ruthless iron.' Richard marries a fine-looking woman called Margaret, who despite the struggles of early married life, will end her days dressed in furs.

The young couple start having children and don't stop. In fact they have 13, born in the 20 years between 1875 and 1895, bringing them up in Frank Place, North Shields (the octogenarian writer can remember the names of all the street's residents). Bob is the last, and the eighth son. The fact that his middle name is therefore Octave, and that of his slightly older brother Septimus, hints at the fact that their father is no ordinary blacksmith. Dick likes a drink but loves poetry, reads Herrick and Pope to his children, and is punctilious about them speaking proper English.

He begins to write poetry himself: one, about his first four children, is called *My Queen and Three Kings*. For the last five years of his life in the 1920s, the *North Shields Daily News* and the *South Shields Gazette* publish every Saturday a poem of Dick's, in Tyneside dialect, (*Clivvor Lads at the Street Corner End, The Way They Catch Sparras in Guetshead, Waitin' For Me Daddy*), for each of which he is paid 10 shillings. These are gathered together and published in a volume inscribed 'Ti the wife' and titled *Over the Anvil*. This little book represents a realisation of the old man's dream to be a writer. Finally he is found dead at his desk, right hand covering his last poem, which is called *Tripped Oot*. His youngest son remembers him fondly: 'A human, matey old boy'.

And so to Dixon, the older brother Bob clearly adored...

Born in 1883, named after his grandmother's maiden name, he shows wit and energy from an early age: he has not one but two paper rounds. He leaves school at 13, and gets a job as junior clerk with the Tyne Iron Shipping Company where he learns shorthand and typing. His leaving testimonial describes him as 'extremely accurate, quick and painstaking, his abilities consistently above the average'. When he is 16, his older brother Thomas, 'handsome, arrogant Tot,' who at 18 had taken the Civil Service exam and found himself posted to the British Consulate in Batoum in Russia, wires Dixon to join him in the potential bonanza of the Baku oilfields. He returns two years later, only a little richer but a good deal wiser. He also brings home the lifelong fascination with Eastern art, culture and religion that will find expression 40 years later in the building of his News Theatre.

According to Bob, he 'falls for the teachings of some jerk called the Mahatma and has my poor mother cooking all kinds of weird dishes. But these are only signs of an experimental and imaginative brain.'

At 21, Dixon enters the booming electricity industry, becoming secretary of the Hexham and District Electric Supply Co. Ltd. Along with Bob's book, Anthea Guthrie has company papers from the early 1900s that indicate its role in the rapid electrification of Newcastle's shops and restaurants, including Tilley's by the Monument, just round the corner from High Friar Lane and the site of the News Theatre Dixon will build 35 years later.

At 25 he marries Virginia Duffell, henceforth known as Virgi. Bob calls her 'the intelligent, elegant and humorous Virgi'. She is a talented pianist, who will later count conductors Adrian Boult and Malcolm Sargent among her friends. Sadly we know nothing of how the newly-weds met, but the Duffells were Irish gentry and so young Dixon clearly made quite a catch in snaffling her. In late Edwardian Tyneside, he seems set fair for a rewarding if conventional life in what's now called the utility industry.

And then his sister Marie pays a visit to Jarrow.

Marie is five years older than Dixon and a talented singer and musician. After teaching violin and voice in Scotland, she'd gone into variety, establishing her own troupe of mostly female singers and musicians, the delightfully named Marie Scott's Caledonian Fisherfolk, who toured Britain's music halls for a generation. Marie herself will eventually die in penury in Brixton, the place where variety artistes traditionally subsided, but in 1908 she is resting at home on Tyneside. Here she comes up with a brilliant idea, gathering together her brothers and sisters (at least those still around) to share it.

She tells them she'd recently visited a bioscope (the word cinema hadn't yet been invented) and seen something that transcended the crude pieces of actuality and comedy skits of the very early films. Here was a real story, with actors who knew what they were about, its exposition helped by caption cards. She tells her family the 'shows' are here to stay, and that they should all give up their jobs, find a hall somewhere and start a business of their own.

Right: Virginia 'Virgi' Scott, Dixon's wife.

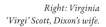

Everyone thinks she's mad, but Marie starts searching for the right premises. Along Grange Road in Jarrow she finds a building that intrigues her. Once a club for workers at Palmer's shipyard, then a Salvation Army hall, wash-house and finally second-hand furniture shop, she explores its interior and finds a space she measures out with her dainty dancer's feet. She works out how many tip-up seats it can accommodate and how much a full house could turn over. She then brings three of her brothers to see it. They dismiss it out of hand, but when she accuses them of being 'hyullies' (local vernacular for cowards), they're stung into looking at Marie's sums further. They're disconcerted to find she's right – it could make money, enough to keep the whole family. And what's more, it's exciting, it's the future – and they all take a great leap into it.

So Harry doesn't go back to sea as a ship's engineer, John Robert (JR) locks his barber's shop and Dixon resigns from his safe and well-paid job at the Hexham and District Electric Supply Co. Ltd. They all pitch in together, hiring shipyard craftsmen to fit out the hall, finding a Pathé Frères projector and an experienced man, Howcroft, to operate it, as well as a local renter in Newcastle who'll provide the films. Only one thing is missing – a name – but after a lengthy family conference, they accept Dixon's suggestion: a shortening of 'kinematograph' – the old word for Pathé's magic box – to four satisfying letters: *Kino*.

It's a clever title, and Dixon is pleased with it, but in time comes to regret it, as he confided in his journal 30 years later: 'The modesty of the title. Yet not a successful one. Did not fit in to the Scottish pronunciation of the word, as I still had to learn that my job was not to teach, but to entertain. I had many expensive lessons, and yet never thoroughly overcame my failing!'

Finally all the preparations are done, and the Kino has its opening night, on 11 September 1908. Dixon manages the business, JR the house, Harry helps Howcroft in the operating box, little Maggie sells tickets in the pay-box, Marie's in charge of the band and at 12 years old, Bob – now Mister Robert – is the general dogsbody. In time, their mother and father, Margaret and Richard, will come to work in the business too, until JR sacks his mother for allowing too many 'barefoot guttersnipes' in for nothing.

That night all 240 seats for both shows were filled – at tuppence, fourpence and sixpence – but the houses soon dropped off, and it required all of Dixon Scott's ingenuity, and the whole family's energy, to turn the Kino into a thriving business.

In the months ahead they tried all kinds of wheezes, many of which disguised the essential nature of cinema – a two-dimensional entertainment that someone has prepared earlier – and harked back to the traditions and trickery of variety. So it was that either JR or Dixon introduced the films – giving them a big build-up – and then 'lectured to them', as the stories unfolded, explaining the finer points of plot and character, as they stood on the stage to the side of the screen. A loud voice came in handy, partly because of the live musical accompaniment. At the Kino, this went far beyond the traditional solo piano. Sister Marie actually led a quartet – pianist, two violinists and cello. There were sound effects too, provided from behind a curtain at one side by two characters called the Chatt Brothers. Bob recalls that in the comedies of the time windows were always being broken, so one of the Chatts put on a kind of iron boot and plunged it into a bucket of broken glass. Gun shots were recreated with a wad of newspapers smacked on a table, horses with coconut shells, and for ocean scenes, a handle was turned on a barrel of peas...

Sometimes I lie in bed wondering whatever happened to the fascinating Chatt Brothers...

Dixon also provided live entertainment between films, including the Tyneside comedian Wal Langtry and 'Walter Conilla, the phenomenal double-voiced vocalist'. On Christmas Night 1908 there was a 'beautiful coloured pantomime story of Cinderella' and each evening that holiday Dixon sang *Merry Christmas* to the audience, which, according to the *Jarrow News*, 'proved exceptionally popular'. Then he began to write songs of his own – a new one every week – that reflected local scenes and events. One celebrated a new order for Palmer's shipyard, but the most popular and enduring was sung by JR to the tune of *The Keel Row*, with its new lyric on the screen. It went:

> *In all the streets of Jarrow, of Jarrow, of Jarrow,*
> *In streets both broad and narrow, the lads and lassies sing,*
> *How happy they all are-o, they are-o, they are-o,*
> *The reason is not far-o,*
> *Just listen what they sing:*
>
> *We've all been to the Kino, the Kino, the Kino,*
> *Where the films are fine-o, the best we've ever seen,*
> *We'll go again to the Kino, the Kino, the Kino,*
> *It's the best place on the Tyne-o,*
> *And cosy, neat and clean.*

THE KINO PICTURE HALL
GRANGE ROAD.
JARROW

BARNES & BURTON
ARCHITECTS - NEWCASTLE

Audiences loved the song, children sang it in the streets. Seven years later young Bob went ashore with invading Allied troops at Cape Helles in the Dardanelles campaign of 1915. As he hit the beach, a soldier nearby copped a bullet and went down. Bob knelt beside him and recognised him from the old Jarrow days. The wounded man smiled and began to sing, 'We'll go again to the Kino, the Kino, the Kino...'

Above: The new Kino Picture Hall, which opened in 1910, from Dixon Scott's advertising brochure 'The Kino and All About It'.

Gradually audiences built, among them, Dixon remembered years later:

'The girls from the haddock shop at the comedy matinee, in their white aprons. Fishermen in from sea, just fresh from danger: full of beer and devilment. Many people come in with their jaws set, plonk themselves in their seats, look defiantly at the stage, say now go on, make me laugh.'

The programme they enjoyed ran for just under two hours and was shown twice nightly. The films – dramas, romances and comedies (Bob especially loved those of the Frenchman Max Linder) – lasted ten minutes each, the time it took to hand-crank 1,000 feet of film, not too fast and not too slow (the film would catch fire if it was in the gate too long). Dixon saw the attraction of local footage, and found a cameraman, a certain Longhorn from Westerhope, who took pictures of pitmen coming out of the local pits and workmen streaming out of Palmer's shipyard. And they and their wives and kids poured into the Kino to see Dad on the pictures. Next up Dixon paid £50 for the exclusive rights to a match between Newcastle and Sunderland and sold the footage on to other cinemas to make a killing.

He's smart, young Mr Scott, dreaming up new schemes in his office over the road from his baby theatre, doing deals on his brand new telephone (he wangles the number Jarrow 111). He soon sees that the way to make a real killing is to increase the hall's capacity. So the old wash-house comes down – there's the suggestion of a fire – and a brand new Kino goes up in its place at a cost of £5,000, the first purpose-built cinema in the North.

For its opening, on 1 August 1910, Dixon writes an advertising brochure – a copy's on the desk in front of me – called *The Kino and All About It*, which the Chatt Brothers distribute around the town. The booklet features pictures of the three older Scott boys, the words of various of Dixon's local songs, and also stresses the suitability of the entertainment to the whole family. An adept phrasemaker is at work here. I like 'Every picture tells a story, and there are 60,000 pictures in every Kino performance', but one sweetly pithy phrase is repeated time and again. It provides me with the title of this book: *Come and See*.

Below: Dixon Scott's advertising wheeze, 'The Kino and All About It'.

The new venture is a big success, and the Scotts soon open a second cinema in nearby Hebburn, calling it the Royal Kino, where they hold talent contests between the films. In 1912 they take over the Theatre of Varieties in Saville Street, North Shields, renaming it the Central Kino, then a cinema in Sunderland called the Villiers, and finally build a new cinema in South Shields, inevitably also named the Kino.

And of course young Dixon Scott never returns to his safe job at the Hexham and District Electric Supply Co. Ltd. It's easy to see why: the business is flying and making money, probably quite a lot. But beyond that, it was clearly an exciting, intoxicating life, and one shared with his beloved brothers and sisters.

The story is like the plot of an MGM musical of the 1930s: you can imagine Judy Garland in it. Then again, that's perhaps the wrong analogy. There's such magic in the story of the Kino and the struggles and inspired ideas of the family running it, this could be an English *Cinema Paradiso* – in Jarrow!

Dixon's future as Tyneside's rising young mogul of 'the shows', as Bob calls them, seems assured. What could possibly go wrong?

But it does, rather horribly. Within two years, pretty much the whole Scott empire comes crashing down.

There are three reasons for this: two are routine aspects of business life, and the other a rather more interesting aspect of Dixon's character. Before the outbreak of the First World War, there is a short, sharp recession and workers are laid off at many of the Tyne's shipyards and engineering works. In addition, there's growing competition from other cinema operators – two other cinemas open in Jarrow alone, the Gem and the Empire. They're not a patch on the Kino, but the trouble is that Dixon won't just give his public what they want – 'the bang-bang and galloping hooves, pratfalls and crude comedy'. He won't just snatch their money. He wants to better their lives, to improve them – that much is clear from the Kino's 'Come and See' brochure. He wants above all to make them think. This turns out to be an impulse that beats for the rest of his life and beyond, in the building of his News Theatre and the policy of the independent cinema that replaced it.

As Bob observes with exasperation: 'This man is not only a businessman but there's a strong streak of idealism there too, and in the commercial world that's often like trying to mix oil with water. He's a prophet, and we all know what happens to prophets, they land up in a cave somewhere starving, with nothing but their long whiskers to keep them warm!'

A sense of Dixon's social mission can be caught in the journal found in the Tyneside skip in the 1980s, from a few lines of rough notes for the novel about the early cinema that was never written (as far as I know).

'How the Cinemas Grew; and why; filled a great social need. Industrial communities; no hobbies, nor possibility of hobbies. *Streets to walk*. Poor. Industrial communities etc. Uneducated. Vision bound. Opened the world to them. A godsend. Greatest *temperance* reform known.'

In pursuit of these ideals, Dixon starts showing classy films from the Continent, being particularly fond of adaptations of classic novels like *Germinal* and *Les Misérables*. There's a problem with the latter – it's two hours long, so Dixon decides to show it in two halves, part one running Monday, Tuesday, Wednesday, and two Thursday, Friday, Saturday. The result is a flop: folk simply can't afford two shows in a week, and consequently go elsewhere.

For the opening night at the South Shields Kino he chooses an early Italian version of Dante's *Inferno*. But the audience of pitmen and their families from St Hilda's Colliery don't find the story sobering and morally improving; when they see the writhing snakes and sinners being tormented in hell, they think it hilarious. Most don't return...

So that picture house folds and a boxing hall replaces it, and Dixon blames its demise on the fact it had 13 shareholders and opened on the 13th of the month. Then the lease on the Hebburn Kino runs out and the owners want to pull it down for redevelopment, and finally just before war breaks out, debts force him to let go of his first-born, the Jarrow Kino. 'And this is a tragedy,' writes Bob, 'because if only we hang on for a few months everybody's employed again and cash flowing freely and every place of entertainment is packed.'

This must have been hard to take, but in 1914 there are greater sufferings in the world. A small rump of Dixon's business remains, and he nurtures it while most of his brothers go off to war (he's ruled out on health grounds). He arranges with Sinclair's of Newcastle for regular parcels of Chevalier cigarettes to be sent to Bob in various theatres of war and painstakingly corrects Forster's errors of spelling and grammar in his letters home.

Dixon Scott has taken a battering, but continues to dream. His initiative in hiring local cameramen and screening footage of local scenes and events in his cinemas has given him a big idea. In 1911 he approaches LNER and asks for space in their Central Station in Newcastle to build a theatre specifically for showing films about regional, national and international news. The railway company doesn't get it – despite the £1,000 offered – and turns the young businessman down.

But it's too good an idea to forget, and eventually, 25 years later, Dixon Scott's final dream is realised – and what a gem this new Kino will be...

Opposite page:
'Broken Blossoms', directed by movie pioneer DW Griffith and starring 'sweet little' Lillian Gish, entranced Dixon Scott's customers at the Comedy cinema, North Shields.

Photo © British Film Institute

3 | 'Laughter and tears; glamour; beauty...'

At the outbreak of the First World War, Dixon Scott regresses somewhat, in more ways than one.

He only has one 'show' left – the little, ramshackle theatre in his home town of North Shields, the Central Kino, a name soon abandoned, perhaps because he comes to believe the snappy four-letter title, much used south of the river, hasn't exactly brought him much luck. In 1914 it becomes the Comedy.

It's a febrile time – down the bank to the Fish Quay, the long-established butcher's shop of Herr Kuch, famed far and wide for his succulent pork sandwiches, is besieged and wrecked by a mob of locals who suddenly don't like his name. But people want entertainment, and they flock to the variety shows put on by Dixon. For the time being he has given up on cinema.

He puts everything into his remaining theatre, booking the acts, advertising and then introducing them on stage, selling them that little bit harder if he thinks they're dodgy. By all accounts he's popular with the artistes, who use the Comedy as a stopping off point before they embark on tours of Scottish halls. He is kind, generous and thoughtful, though sharp with the comics if their material strays towards 'smut'. Tyneside comics like Wal Langtry, Harry Harvey and JC Scatter are hugely popular. Many of these acts are booked in London by Bob Scott, who haunts the pubs of Brixton where many old pros hang out, and here he finds a singer down on his luck, one Tom Costello, famed for his song *At Trinity Church I Met My Doom,* and offers him a sub of £5 against four weeks' work, much of which Bob and Dixon sell on at a profit to other halls. The two remaining brothers in the business seem remarkably adept at such ducking and diving, though Dixon develops a distaste for at least some of the entertainment he sells so successfully.

From the journal in the skip:

'The appalling slushiness of many popular songs... proves that the public not only devour tripe with gusto and digest it with avidity, but also that they like it in concentrated form. Give them a heart that is true under skies of blue with a lilt or soothing sway in the melody, and they fairly gobble it. This goes on from generation to generation, without alteration, without improvement. The number of "*jazz*" songs which have used up this true and tried form of tripe can never be counted, and yet they are no worse than the song which was responsible for the great popularity of the musical comedy, *The Maid of the Mountains*.'

It's maybe for this reason then that at the end of the war, Dixon abandons variety and dips his toe again into the shark-infested waters of the cinema business. Despite local competition from the modern Albion and the Boro, owned by legendary showman George Black, whose son will go on to manage the London Palladium, Dixon converts the tiny 550-seat Comedy to moving pictures. To survive he must use his wits more cleverly than ever before – and really *sell*.

An example. In 1919 a film set in London's Chinatown is released. *Broken Blossoms* is a powerful drama directed by the movie pioneer DW Griffith and starring Richard Barthelmess and 'sweet little' Lillian Gish, who's destined for stardom. Dixon manages to get the film, but not on an exclusive – something special is required. The film's title gives him an idea. He commissions local artist Gerald Dorman to paint a special 'flat' in flaming reds and despatches Bob to Huddersfield where he buys £100 worth of imitation blossoms in many colours. So as the audience settle in their seats, they gaze not at the blank screen but at the picturesque flat, and then the blossoms fall slowly from the ceiling onto 550 upturned, enraptured faces. They sigh with pleasure – the scruffy little theatre in North Shields has become a kind of fairyland. Only then do the lights go down, the flat is removed and the story flickers into life. There is not a sound in the house.

So Dixon Scott is getting his confidence back, if indeed he ever lost it. He slowly builds up the empire again, more slowly and surely this time. In the town of Prudhoe, west of Newcastle, Dixon investigates two shows, fighting for the same custom and cutting each other's throats as a result, so he buys both, sells one to a group wanting to open a workingmen's club, and keeps the other, which he names the Electric, perhaps in wry tribute to his former occupation. The Electric is managed by his older brother JR, until he leaves to run his own cinema on the Scotswood Road in Newcastle. The Electric will provide a steady income for Dixon for the next 20 years.

He then pulls off a similar trick in the supposedly unlucky territory of South Shields, where he buys the Imperial in Tyne Dock. There's competition nearby – and times are again hard as the Twenties stagger on – so he approaches the management of the opposition and offers to close the Imperial as a cinema and sell it for another purpose, if they'll give him £2,000. He gets it.

Not always however. In his journal he recalls the wiles of a 'renter' from whom he sometimes took films:

'Salesmanship:
Moppy Middlebrook and his company: the lovely and clever Jewess who helped him in his office. During arguments about booking the films and their prices she would draw her stocking suspender tight and let it slap back upon her legs. There was no impropriety, she was as straight as a die and except for taking too much drink, so was he, but the slapping of the suspenders on her bare legs had a devastating effect upon one's morale, and for a while the exhibitor was ready to sign on the dotted line almost at any price.'

But it seems Dixon is beginning to tire of all this hustling, and the consequent strain on him and his family life – by now Virgi has given birth to three sons, as he confides in his journal:

'Running Cinemas:
Hard work. Incessant alertness. George Black and other showmen not having their Sundays. He is a very successful man, but I doubt whether he ever rests. The penalty of never seeing family. No games. Nervous strain. The twice-weekly change. How it is effected.'

At the grand old age of 45 he decides to do it differently, to stop scratching around and go for broke. He painstakingly acquires small parcels of land on a site in North Shields and then builds a spanking new and capacious cinema, which he calls the Prince's; it opens in October 1929. It is a palace, but don't take my word for it...

The Town and Country News of June 1930 reports that the cinema 'has won enormous popularity for its comfort and high class programming. No expense was spared in this palatial cinema – café, grand organ on which Mr Leslie Ord is a real artist and accompanies silent films as well as playing requests from the audience.' *Kinematograph Weekly* is equally enthusiastic: 'The artistic scheme of decoration throughout the theatre is in the Oriental style, as designed by the architect (George Bell of Dixon and Bell). The fibrous plaster work was carried out by the Decorative Plaster Co. of Newcastle and the decorative panels in marblecote are the work of M. Alexander, art master of Newcastle.'

The Alexander brothers (yet more brothers) decorated many Tyneside cinemas, using bold colours and abstract, stylised decorative forms. The Prince's made extravagant use of art deco style – fibrous plaster wall decorations, combed plaster work and cellulose sprayed on walls in graduated tones, the whole effect modulated by the manipulation of coloured lights. This kind of sunny elegance was much appreciated by the customers, probably because their own homes were often drab, dark and rather dingy.

The Prince's isn't Dixon's for long. Eager to build up their circuit, Gaumont British make him an offer he can't refuse and he moves on to his next project, the Haymarket in Newcastle. Designed by George Bell, the same architect responsible for the Prince's, the Haymarket is again in the art deco style, but Dixon's influence is growing. Indeed, it's claimed to be based on a cinema in Cairo he once visited and liked. Friezes of palm trees and camels in the foyer welcome patrons into the 1,280-seat cinema. With the interior styled again by one of the Alexander brothers, it's opened in December 1933 by comedian Tom Walls, star of the first-night film *Just Smith*, which is screened after various shorts and songs from the Prudhoe Gleemen.

Dixon still has a soft spot for what his brother Bob calls 'weird films'.

In 1934, a history master at Heaton Grammar School called Ernest Dyer got together with a group of like-minded souls and set up the Tyneside Film Society, to show the best 'minority interest' films in Newcastle. Looking for a home, they approached Dixon Scott and he allowed them to use the Haymarket for their screenings (until 1940, when they moved to the News Theatre). The very first film to be shown was *Sous les Toits de Paris*, René Clair's touching musical comedy. Foreign films and documentaries provided the bulk of the fare, along with classic Hollywood movies, a combination bound to appeal to Dixon Scott, who 25 years earlier had often programmed Italian and German films at his first tiny cinema in Jarrow, the beginning of his lifelong commitment to education and 'improvement'.

Dixon hasn't changed. He often books movies with a literary flavour, including a version of Cervantes' *Don Quixote*. This arrives in Newcastle hardly trailing clouds of glory, offered by the distributors at a nominal sum and easy to see why: it is, says, Bob Scott, 'the most horrible bit of cheese you can possibly imagine'. He fears it will bomb, and on opening night fortifies himself with two double-Scotches in the Crow's Nest next door. He need not have feared: his brother gets up on stage to introduce the film and pulls off a piece of the old magic, hypnotising the audience, including the critic of the *Evening Chronicle*, into believing they're about to see something very special, which of course they do. *Don Quixote* does great business.

Dixon still has a bee in his bonnet about news. At the Haymarket he screens *News of the North*, a regular feature compiled by local cameramen – one early item features an empty Northumberland reservoir during the drought of 1934, the film being processed in London after Dixon has a word with his contacts at Universal. This service doesn't last long – it proves too costly – but Dixon stores the experience for later and embarks on another plan: to increase the capacity to 2,000, to provide the financial muscle to turn the Haymarket into a 'first-run' cinema (showing the big films before anyone else), but finding someone else to take the risk. When the cinema is reopened in August 1936 with a screening of the Marx Brothers' *A Night at the Opera*, he has already leased the cinema for 21 years to Associated British Pictures. The white-fronted Haymarket becomes the ABC, Dixon pockets the risk-free income of £4,500 a year and embarks on his most ambitious project yet. It will also be his last...

In fact he's been quietly working on his News Theatre for three or four years, and dreaming of it for 25.

In 1935, just as he lets go of the day-to-day management of the Haymarket, Dixon calls brother Bob into his office and tells him about his plans. They discuss where to put the new venture, spreading a large scale Ordnance Survey map of the city on the desk in front of them. Bob suggests the site of the Louis Café at the top of Northumberland Street – roughly where the opposition to come, the Tatler News Theatre, will spring up – but Dixon's finger moves 200 yards to the south, encircling a frontage on Pilgrim Street, with High Friar Lane to the side. The plot is more central, close to the heart of the city at Grey's Monument, near the department stores of Fenwick, Binns and Bainbridge's, between the bus stations at Haymarket and Worswick Street and barely 10 minutes' walk from the Central Station. It turns out of course to be the perfect location. There are several small shops on the site, but Dixon thinks he can repeat the same stunt he pulled off in North Shields, assembling the land he needs piecemeal, buying out the shops on the site separately, as well as acquiring the back yard of Smart's Furnishers in Grey Street.

Below: George Bell, the architect commissioned by Dixon Scott to realise his grand vision for Newcastle's News Theatre.

Which is exactly what he does. He again engages Newcastle architect George Bell, by now a trusted collaborator, to design the theatre. Bell is an established architect with a flourishing regional practice, a sober man who travels by tram every day from his large house in Reid Park Road, Jesmond (complete with garden house he built for his daughter) to his office in Northumberland Street, leather briefcase in hand and spats on his shoes.

But if he provides the frame for the News Theatre, it is Dixon who paints the picture. The rich detailing – Persian on an art deco design – isn't in the plans drawn up by Bell, but instead conceived by Dixon, the self-confessed 'passionate orientalist' who constructs this latest fantasy world from his library of books on art and design and various tours of the Middle East, where he has spent many hours in the great mosques of Istanbul and the epic buildings of Cairo and Teheran.

The entrance to the cinema was then a stylish arcade 54 feet long, featuring mosaic and terrazzo floor, marble walls, neon tubing, decoration in fibrous plaster and a pay-box in granite, marble and stainless steel. The work was carried out by two local firms: the Decorative Plaster Company and the Commercial Carpet and Tile Company, who were sub-contractors to the builder, Thomas Clements. Dixon knew Charles Holmes, proprietor of Commercial Carpet and Tile – they were both members of the Pen and Palette Club in nearby Higham Place – and they spent many hours discussing how to achieve what Dixon wanted. In the end Holmes bought beam compasses to set out the mosaic floor patterns and employed Italian craftsmen to do the work. Dixon stood over them as they worked. He even chose the colours of the painted detailing.

So Dixon gets what he wants: a monument to Islamic art and the culture of film, and perhaps to himself. He is written all over the building, which even includes in its main theatre the gilded proscenium arch of a music hall, where he began his career in show business 30 years earlier. But there are modern comforts and the latest technology: the 252 seats in the stalls, and the 162 in the balcony, are filled with Dunlopillo cushioning, there's an RCA sound system, a Lumaplak screen and projection equipment supplied by Cowe and Co Ltd, including provision for the expected transmission by the BBC shortly of television programmes to theatres.

So to opening day: Monday 1 February 1937. Snowy weather threatens to prevent it, but workmen labour through the night to finish off the roof. Guests and civic dignitaries are greeted by a fanfare of trumpets for the first performance, the proceeds of which will go to the Fleming Hospital for Sick Children. Jean McPherson, a patient there, gives a bouquet of lilacs to the Lady Mayoress, Mrs John Grantham, whose husband is escorted to the stage by Dixon to make his speech.

The opening programme includes newsreels from Gaumont British, Fox Movietone and Universal, a Mickey Mouse cartoon called *Moving Day* and a film called *Gentlemen in Top Hats and Gentlemen in Crowns* about changes in British pageantry over the last 25 years. All goes well, and Dixon confides to a correspondent from *Kinematograph Weekly*, 'If the theatre is half full the whole time I shall be well content.'

As things turn out, it does very much better than that – as we shall see – but Dixon doesn't live to see it. During the negotiations to lease the Haymarket to ABC, according to letters between him and the company, he'd frequently taken time off work due to illness. Once the News Theatre is up and running, he starts planning a delayed return visit to Egypt. He and Virgi want to visit the antiquities at Aswan, but before leaving Cairo Dixon feels unwell and a doctor sends him to the Anglo-American Hospital to rest.

Below and opposite page: The exotic splendour of Dixon Scott's News Theatre.

He dies a week later, on 11 February 1939, his youngest son Ridley at his bedside, and is later buried in Alexandria. Family legend has it that the last crisis was brought on by a bout of the hiccups. He was 55.

Typically, Dixon had the foresight to plan his succession before he died. He'd set up a new company to run the News Theatre and his ownership of the Haymarket and the Prudhoe Electric. He called it Haridix Ltd. For weeks I wonder about the name before I work it out. The name is an amalgam of the first names of his three sons – Harry (named after Virgi's brother, killed on the Western Front during the First World War), Ridley and Dixon Junior, who are all, with Virgi, directors of the company. He also asked his eldest, named after himself, to manage the News Theatre. Later I discover the company's trademark, designed by the boys' father: three hands clasped together in brotherly love and allegiance.

At Dixon Senior's death, his own younger brother Bob lost his mentor, guide and teacher. In his memoir, 'the last and least' of the family Scott pays tribute to his nurturing, and thanks him for buying him *Scouting for Boys* and countless other books, and for paying to get his wonky teeth fixed.

'You do all these things for me Dixon, nobody else does,' says Robert Forster Octave Scott.

With his brother gone, Bob couldn't face staying on Tyneside, and took a job managing the Forum in Liverpool, the beginning of three decades of wandering from town to town, cinema to cinema, that finally ended in that 'dingy flat third floor back' a few minutes from Brighton's sea front, where the old man finally wrote down his story.

There's another epitaph, this time written by Dixon Scott himself, of his amazing, comic and poignant role in the growth of 'the shows' in this small corner of England. In his elegant shorthand in the journal rescued from a skip outside the last cinema he built, the cinema that was the best expression of his values and tastes, he wrote these words:

Below: Illustrations from 'Bhartrihari Says', a book of Sanskrit poetry translated into English by polymath and 'passionate orientalist' Dixon Scott.

'We are the Aunt Sallies, the cock-shies, of all the little lads who can afford a penny ball to throw at us, but amongst us, we have built up a business for the public that all the highbrows and their allies cannot kill. Laughter and tears; glamour; beauty. The screen killed the ungainly garb of women, and dressed them as daintily and becomingly as they are now. Yes, my bonny lads and lassies, we do all that for you...'

Dixon Scott

'Brainy little man, gentle little man, tough little man, beloved little man.'

Dixon Scott, founder father of the Tyneside Cinema, may have dominated the last two chapters of this book, but we aren't yet done with him – or perhaps more correctly, he's not done with us.

The scope of his short life is such that there's only been space so far to describe his career in the cinema trade, culminating in the building of his Persian picture palace at the top of Pilgrim Street.

But he did so much else in his 55 years that they demand to be acknowledged. Just stick with me for a few moments...

At the age of 23 he published his first novel, *Zarya: A Tale of the Caucasus*, published by John Long at 10 shillings, presumably based on his travels in southern Russia a few years earlier; the book received a warm notice in *The Times*. He wrote two other novels, one set in Pity Me, Durham, another, a thriller called *The 49 Pound Pike*, in Finland. He planned to write one based on his life in cinema called *The White Spot*, but sadly there's no evidence he got beyond the planning stage.

Dixon was a passionate and prolific poet. Some of his poems were published in *Punch*. A collection he put together himself includes *The Minstrel's Lament*, *To a June Bride* and some verse 'scribbled at Quaglino's as the Prince of Wales danced before us'; he and Virgi were dining with the distinguished painter, Dame Laura Knight. His brother Bob preferred poems on Northumbrian themes (Dixon was, like his father, an enthusiastic supporter and speaker of its dialect); Bob most fondly remembered verses on Thomas Bewick and *The Fifer of the Fifth*, about soldiers in the Northumberland Fusiliers. Many of these poems were written in Dixon's few idle moments towards the end of his life, on the train between Newcastle and the family home facing the North Sea, on the elegant curve of Percy Gardens in Tynemouth.

The showman was also an enthusiastic traveller, picking up languages as well as ideas for cinema decor. These linguistic skills he put to impressive use, translating a volume of Sanskrit poetry by the 1st century BC master Bhartrihari into English (published after his death), as well as songs later broadcast on the BBC in Finnish, another difficult language to learn.

Mr. DIXON SCOTT.

Full-sized reproductions of these caricatures printed on Art Paper, suitable for framing, may be had on application to the publishers.

He wrote many songs of his own, many of them sung from the stages of his cinemas by him or his brother, JR.

Some of his literary efforts had a more private purpose: he once wrote a lullaby for his infant son Ridley and a poem full of tender advice in the style of Polonius, *To My Son Dixon, on his leaving home to go to Stratford Grammar School, May 4th 1925*: 'Be generous, not mean. Bear no revenge,' he tells him, before finishing with the heartfelt, 'And by your side I'll stand, for you against the world, I love you, son'.

He bequeathed his sons more than just a substantial living, passing on a repugnance for 'smut' and 'loose morals', encouraged as he thought by the pervasive influence of American culture, which was certainly shared by his oldest son Dixon. The father was an enthusiastic writer of letters to the newspapers, from *The Times* to *Kinematograph Weekly*, on these and other issues of the day. Not surprisingly, he was a lifelong Tory and whole-hearted Mason. What's more surprising perhaps is how much sympathy he retained for the working man, and the steps he took to show it.

Among the effects inherited by his grand-daughter Phillipa Turnbull is an exquisite coloured testimonial, given by the United Society of Boilermakers and Iron and Steel Shipbuilders, 'presented to Mr Dixon Scott, proprietor of the Kino Theatre, Jarrow by the Executive Council for his many kindnesses to the members of the Society in Jarrow during the lock-out of 1910'. 25 years later he made generous contributions to a fund supporting the Jarrow marchers.

Dixon Scott then was a man both compassionate and passionate, about many things. At every point in a life cut short he was a man in a hurry, seemingly filling every waking moment with the expression of his personality, gulping down every kind of experience life put before him.

The anonymous obituarist put it well: 'His career was one of constant action and movement.'

I wonder where this drive came from. Was it that cliché, the ambition of the bright working-class lad made good?

Well, yes.

But in the end it turns out the truth is more complicated.

Opposite page: A caricature of Dixon Scott published in 'Northern Lights' on 6 April 1920. The artist, Gerald Dorman, painted a special set for Scott's screening of 'Broken Blossoms' in 1919.

Back in 1899, when 'handsome, arrogant Tot' sent for him to go to Batoum and he embarked on a Baltic tramp steamer on the first stage of an endless journey to the Caucasus, he hoped to get rich in Russia's first great oil boom. What he got instead was ill, very ill.

He contracted what was then called Bright's Disease, now known as nephritis, an acute condition of the kidneys, which causes stones in those organs and is acutely painful. At that time there was no known cure, and sufferers usually died. Indeed the matchless, beautiful Jean Harlow died of it the year the News Theatre opened. One can hardly imagine what medical care was like in a frontier town on the edge of Russia in 1900, but certainly the 16-year-old boy was given up for dead. The fact that he didn't die was down to luck – and the care given him by an English nurse called Miss Stevens. For years afterwards they corresponded warmly, and he sent her regular gifts, including an embroidered bed jacket that pleased her greatly. Somehow Dixon survived his ordeal, but there was a catch.

His brush with Bright's Disease damaged a valve in Dixon's heart – the reason why he gave up smoking and drinking, was spared war service, embraced mystical eastern philosophy and became increasingly unwell in his early fifties.

Maybe this was also the reason why he looks so anxious in that photo on the wall of the Tyneside stair. He was a sharp man and surely must have realised he was likely to die early.

'A career of constant movement and activity...'

Spare a thought then for poor Dixon, as he stood in the foyer of his last great project, the fullest expression of his search for beauty, having let go of the Haymarket and the Prince's, watching those Italian craftsmen piece together the sparkling mosaic floor of his News Theatre, tile by tiny tile.

It was his swansong, and I think he knew it.

Opposite page:
Cinema usherette Molly Hutton poses on right with her pals in High Friar Lane at the beginning of World War II.

Courtesy of Molly Alexander

4 | In Which We Serve

As in so much else, when it came to the concept of a news theatre, Dixon Scott was something of a visionary. It was in 1911 that he saw in film a way to broaden the access to news and current affairs that up till then had been limited to those with the time, money and inclination to read newspapers.

It wasn't for another 15 years – and the joining of sound to the moving image – that others began to see its potential. The very first news cinema opened in New York in 1929, and in the same year the Gaumont-British Movietone News Theatre appeared in Shaftesbury Avenue. Alister MacDonald, son of Prime Minister Ramsay MacDonald, finally picked up on the idea Dixon Scott had for the Central Station 20 years earlier and designed news theatres in London's Victoria and Waterloo stations, opening in 1933-34. The first provincial theatre opened its doors in Birmingham in 1932, and Newcastle followed suit in 1937 with not one but three news theatres opening in the same year.

Scott's theatre was first out of the blocks, opening in February, followed in December by the brand-new Tatler, 150 yards up Northumberland Street, and the Grainger 150 yards the other way in Grainger Street, which had been converted from an existing cinema. It couldn't handle the competition and lasted less than a year, resuming normal programming in 1938, but the Tatler, smaller and less opulent than Dixon's enterprise, stayed the course, actually outliving the News Theatre by a year before finally closing in November 1969.

These cinemas soon found a similar pattern of transmission. The News Theatre opened at 10.30am, with its last performance at 9.30pm. Initially the programme lasted 75 minutes, including three newsreels, the latest cartoons and special sport and travel films. In the early days Dixon Scott had a typical showman's trick up his sleeve – an early form of 3D. 'The great hit of the programme,' read the publicity, 'will be audioscopics – the new stereoscopic film entertainment in which people throw balls, push ladders and squirt soda right up within an inch of your nose – or at any rate you think they do'.

The programme was continuous, so customers could and did come and go. This appealed to shoppers, workers between shifts, people waiting for buses or trains and in later years, students between lectures. Admission was sixpence in the stalls and one shilling in the circle.

Opposite page: Dixon Scott's Press Advertisments Journal – actually a Boots The Chemist Scribbling Diary – which on page 45 lists the takings of both the News Theatre and its rival, The Tatler.

A snapshot: in the cinema archive I found a book containing the cinema's programme in 1938, its first full year. Opposite is what was shown in the week beginning 26 May 1938, as billed in the *Evening Chronicle*.

26 THURSDAY (146-219)

Ascension Day   Holy Thursday   Queen Mary born, 1867

27 FRIDAY (147-218)

28 SATURDAY (148-217)
Removal Term (Scotland)

TAILER.

N · 82 · 7 0

H 22 17 0

£105 4 0

ourselves
£ 272 . 13 . 2 .

The book also records the theatre's receipts for the week: £272, 13 shillings and 2 pence, compared to the Tatler's £105, 4 shillings – a consistent pattern for that year. It is not clear how Scott and his oldest son, also Dixon, then the cinema's manager, managed to get hold of the Tatler's figures, but not entirely surprising that they did.

Interesting too that the newsreels come bottom of the list. In these early years it seems the cinema had access to three – British Movietone, Pathé and Universal, which changed twice a week. Later on there were five, but the News Theatre didn't screen them separately. When they arrived, Dixon Scott Junior would view them and then assemble them into one segment, to avoid repetition and to suit local tastes. His daughters also remember him, in later years, cutting out any material he thought might offend his audience, especially 'the ladies'. At the end of their run, one of the projectionists would have the tedious task of breaking apart the assembly and returning its parts to the original newsreels before they were returned. It isn't clear if the companies knew about this – perhaps it was common practice?

This editing work was carried out in the cinema's 'lecture theatre', on the third floor, the space now occupied by the Roxy. This boasted slide lantern, epidiascope (for projecting images of objects, books and drawings onto a screen), grand piano, 16mm cinematograph apparatus and 'water and gas for chemical experiments'. Dixon Scott's zeal for 'improvement' was clearly still as strong as ever. In 1938 the cinema also began transmitting matinees of educational films, especially on history and geography. These included a study of Highland crofting, *Men of the Alps*, the history of railways and 'the development of the franchise since 1832', appropriate given the close proximity of the Monument to Earl Grey, moving spirit of that year's Reform Act.

Below: The Tyneside Coffee Rooms as photographed by the magazine 'Geordie Life', circa 1938.

A more accidental development was the Coffee Rooms. Originally Dixon Scott Senior had planned another use for this space on the second floor, conscious of the many tailors and dress shops in Grey Street. He hoped it might appeal to them as a cutting or fitting room, but the rent of £150 a year put them off and he couldn't let it.

It was his wife Virgi who apparently suggested a café – a common feature of cinemas in those days (there was one at the Haymarket, for instance, let to the local baker, Carricks). So the Coffee Rooms came into being and soon established its own clientele separate from but linked to the cinema's. The two institutions, with a few gaps here and there, have enjoyed a mutually supportive and symbiotic relationship ever since. In its promotional literature, there's a phrase that jumps out as pure Dixon Scott, masterly phrasemaker: 'The eggs we serve are not yet laid'. To this day, poached eggs on toast and fried egg and chips remain two of the Coffee Room's most enduring and popular of offerings.

There were two rooms nearby reserved for more privileged customers – the Tyne Room, with its painted frieze of river scenes (now the Digital Lounge) and the Smoke Room, both used mainly by gentlemen and businessmen and their wives. As a result these rooms enjoyed a more personal and speedier service. A sense of their clientele can be caught from the newspapers and periodicals supplied for customers: the local and national papers, *The Catholic Herald*, *The Humorist* and *Geographical* magazine were available in the Coffee Rooms; the *Hexham Courant* and *The Countryman* give the Tyne Room a more rural flavour, while the Smoke Room offered more utilitarian periodicals like *The Navy*, the *Chamber of Commerce Journal* and *Blackwood's*.

In the early years of the cinema one of the waitresses in the private rooms was a young woman called Molly Hutton, who after learning shorthand and typing at the commercial school, Skerry's College, on Ellison Place, got a job making gas masks at a factory in Heaton. Here she met a man who was a commissionaire at the News Theatre and he told her the cinema was looking for usherettes. An interview was arranged with the cinema's elderly general manager, Mr Storey, who was always dressed in a morning coat. Molly was taken on and provided with a smart 'Alpine' uniform of her own: apple green blouse and russet red waistcoat and skirt, short to the knee. The cinema paid for Molly and her pals to have a monthly perm and also provided artificial silk stockings, which featured in a daily ritual, as she recalls:

'The owner was a Mrs Scott, she was a widow and she had three sons – Captain Scott in the army, a naval officer was the second son and the other one still at university. Very smart young men. Captain Scott was in charge of the staff in the News Theatre. Anyway he was very, very nice, but he was like a Sergeant Major when he examined us every day – we had to stand in a row while he saw that your stocking seams were straight. We all wore suspenders then. You had to be very, very smart and he marched up and down with his hands behind his back to make sure'.

Molly must have been a trusted employee because apart from working as an usherette and later as a waitress in the Coffee Rooms, she was also sent to spy on the opposition up the road: 'Well, the Tatler wasn't much competition, but it was competition. I think they were more frivolous than we were. So I came back and told Mr Storey, we are much better!'

She was right. When Ossie Nicholson and his family made the pilgrimage from their Gateshead home to the theatre to see the Coronation of King George VI in 1937, they were all mightily impressed by the fact that the footage was in colour.

Customers came from all social classes, and they were allowed to stay for as long as they liked, including sweethearts who occupied the cinema's double seats, little realising that though it was dark, the usherettes' eyesight were used to it. Molly Hutton, soon to marry and join the Women's Auxiliary Air Force, but then 'innocent as the driven snow', hereby received a different kind of education from the coverage of current affairs she saw on the screen.

When wartime came, there was a more compelling reason to keep eyes on the screen. Increasing numbers of servicemen were called up, and their loved ones flocked to the News Theatre to see for themselves what was happening in the many theatres of war. Among them was Virgi, widow of Dixon Scott Senior: all three of her sons went to join the war effort. There's a story behind this – in the history of the Tyneside Cinema, there usually is. Dixon and Virgi had travelled to Germany in 1936 for the Berlin Olympics, and saw for themselves what Nazi fascism was about. Dixon returned home convinced there would soon be war and encouraged Harry, Ridley and Dixon Junior to join the Territorials and Naval Reserve before it began. This wasn't entirely motivated by patriotism. He felt they'd stand more chance of survival if they became officers. He was proved right. They all came home after the war.

Veronica Waters, who grew up in a flat above the Royal Arcade further down Pilgrim Street, has vivid memories of the cinema in wartime:

'It was always very busy, but because the programme was continuous people were always coming and going. You were allowed to stand at the back until a seat became free. My mother worked as a policewoman, but also helped my grandparents who worked at Young's Linen shop in the Royal Arcade as well as acting as caretakers. They were always sewing. I can remember more than once Mother leaning against the wall at the back of the theatre while we waited for seats and just falling asleep with exhaustion. I had to wake her up. Poor Mother.'

Many in the audience were schoolboys, keen to see and hear more about the conflict. Like many others, Charlie Hall from Whitley Bay was often parked in the cinema while his mother went shopping, but he had a personal interest in the war: the Nazis had invaded Poland on his fifth birthday. He believes 'wartime shaped my young life'.

Ossie Nicholson was especially shocked to hear of the sinking of the British battleship HMS Hood in 1941 because he'd seen it in the Tyne before the war, painted salmon pink and looking vast and indestructible. Only later did he discover that some of its armour plating had been removed to make it faster. It sank in three minutes and only three of its 1,400-man crew survived.

David Ramsbotham, whose father was Vicar of St George's, Jesmond, went to the News Theatre every Saturday morning by himself on the trolley bus from Osborne Road. He came from a military family and played war games in Jesmond Dene, his imagination fired by what he saw in the newsreels:

'As long as I live, I'll never forget those very dramatic images in the newsreels of the Battle of El Alamein – the great guns of our artillery firing in the darkness, our soldiers fixing bayonets before going over the top.'

Above: Into battle at El Alamein.

Many remember this footage, but there were many other unforgettable sequences: survivors returning from Dunkirk, the Battle of Britain and the Blitz.

John Charlewood remembers being gripped by the sinking of the German battleship Graf Spee, a documentary about RAF bombers called *Target for Tonight,* and the irony of watching travelogues at a time when everywhere in the world was totally inaccessible.

Below: Jesmond schoolboy and future soldier, David Ramsbotham.

Courtesy of Lord Ramsbotham

When footage from the D-Day landings was shown, David Ramsbotham spotted a house at the head of one of the landing sites – it turned out to be Gold Beach. It was badly damaged by shellfire, but he saw the letters 'TT' crudely painted on the frontage and realised that the 50th Infantry (Tyne-Tees) Division had passed that way. The following year he was given a treat by his parents before returning to the boarding school at Featherstone Castle near Haltwhistle where German POWs worked in the grounds: a visit to the News Theatre, followed by tea around the corner at Tilley's Café. On the way there, they saw a newspaper placard that made them all stop and stare: War In Europe Over.

For all of these young people, the war was brought closer to home by an object that more or less filled the first-floor landing of the News Theatre: a giant free-standing globe. This was one of Dixon Scott's educational initiatives – and he'd paid dearly for it: the cost in 1936 was £52, the equivalent of £2,000 at today's prices. But it provided enduring fascination to Scott's customers, children especially. During wartime they loved to spin it around to find battlefields, places where their loved ones had been posted or even just their home-town. As a consequence, Jean Murray recalls, the surface of the globe was covered in dirty finger marks – and Tyneside more or less obliterated.

Above: The Globe, one of Dixon Scott's educational initiatives, was consulted by thousands of Tynesiders during World War II.

Ossie Nicholson had a very personal reason for examining the globe, specifically the Mediterranean. His brother had been killed on Crete. He also remembers looking for Tobruk after seeing footage of the great battle of the North African campaign in 1942. Shots of German and Italian POWs, ragged and disconsolate, made him believe the Allies would win the war after all.

But of all the images of war screened at the News Theatre during those years, there is one that sticks in the minds of all those who saw it: the liberation of the concentration camps, beginning with Belsen. Veronica Waters was among a packed audience one afternoon:

'It was watched in complete silence. I remember people trudging out at the end, still not speaking, their heads bowed. I can see those images today, I've never forgotten them. I was only 11, but I think it was good for people to see the terrible things the Nazis had done, which our soldiers had stopped.'

(Intriguingly, the camera with which it's thought British Movietone News film-maker Paul Wyand shot this footage, later presented as evidence in the Nuremberg war-crimes trials, is on show in the Tyneside's heritage display on the second floor.)

After the war David Ramsbotham began a long and distinguished career in the services that included commanding a division, directing the Army's public relations during the Falklands War and becoming a general as well as a peer. Now Lord Ramsbotham, he recalls the quality of the war coverage as well as its value for the war effort.

'The commentary was of course jingoistic, but people recognised that and took it with a pinch of salt. But the images were graphic and powerful, far better than actually what we managed 40 years later in the Falklands, and really cemented the war effort on the home front. It was inspiring to see what our troops were doing and why.'

There was one last major event of the war to be played out on the News Theatre's screen – the nuclear attacks on Hiroshima and Nagasaki that brought victory against Japan. Lord Ramsbotham remembers seeing the aerial footage of the two devastated cities: mile after mile of rubble, no sign of any people. It made a great impression on him.

'I couldn't make sense of it at the time – what could have caused this? It was rather frightening, even to an 11-year-old, but now of course I see that it was a turning point in technology and warfare. Things would never quite be the same again.'

But that thought was pushed away in the universal happiness at conflict ending and soldiers returning. For the Scotts, the family running the News Theatre, this pleasure and relief was postponed somewhat, as Dixon Scott Junior didn't return from his wartime service as a Major in the Northumberland Fusiliers until 1947. Until then his mother Virgi continued to mind the show, happy in the knowledge that the News Theatre – and the newsreels it screened – had played a crucial part not only in keeping people informed of the events of war, in bad times as well as good, but in maintaining morale on the home front. Dixon Scott Senior had always known his cinema would find a social purpose – and almost immediately after its opening, during six of the most critical years in Britain's history, he'd been proved right.

As for his customers, Tynesiders had found a place they grew to love. The News Theatre had become an important part of their lives, especially in helping to make them well-informed citizens, and there seemed no reason at all why that should ever change.

Below: Newsreel unit goes to war.

Photo © BUFVC

Heini Przibram

'A great prodder...'

In August 1938, just over a year before the start of World War II, the News Theatre advertised its programme for the week beginning the 22nd.

Alongside *White Magic*, an item on winter sports, 'including a reindeer harnessed to a trap in skis', filmed in the Austrian Tyrol, there was a rather more chilling report from the same part of Europe.

Dixon Scott Junior, director and manager – his father had died earlier that year – wrote: 'May we specially draw your attention to the film *Nazi Conquest of Austria*. This is a natural sequel to the film, *Inside Nazi Germany*, recently shown by us. The course of events in Austria and Germany is graphically described and illustrated, including the long preparations for the Nazi invasion southwards, and the consequent trepidation now experienced by neighbouring states.'

The Austrian Anschluss changed the life, among those of many others, of one young Austrian Jew, who found refuge, education and family in a smoky industrial city in the north of England. And Newcastle's News Theatre – and his passion for the cinema – became a central part of that new life for the next 35 years. But whatever he took from the city, its film culture especially, Heinrich Przibram returned with interest.

The young man's father was a professor of physics in Vienna, but his wider family was steeped in the theatre and cinema. His grandfather, Otto Tressler, made his acting debut in the movies in 1915 and a valedictory appearance at the Burgtheater in Vienna in 1962. His Uncle Georg was a prolific director and writer, and another uncle directed at the Burgtheater.

Heinrich loved the movies too, but he wanted to be a scientist like his father. For a year before the Anschluss, Professor Przibram tried to get his family out of Austria – for the country's Jews, the writing was quite literally on the wall. The USA wouldn't take them on the grounds of his age – he was over 60. Eventually he and Heini's stepmother spent the war years in Belgium, while their 18-year-old son made his own great escape, flying out of Vienna on the very day the Nazis invaded.

Opposite page: Heini Przibram with film director Anthony Asquith, (inset right) on a visit to the Tyneside Film Society in the mid Fifties.

Courtesy of Rommi Przibram

Landing at Croydon, after an anxious wait while an immigration officer phoned an Oxford scientist friend of Heinrich's father to check his credentials, he was finally allowed entry, and eventually to continue his education at King's College, Newcastle. And it was here one day, in a corridor, that he met a tall young woman from South Shields called Rosamonde Crabbe.

More than 70 years later, she tells me down the line from the Welsh borders what happened next.

'He was studying engineering and I was studying chemistry and physics, one of only two female students in the science faculty. We met because engineers and chemists were taught physics together, so I met him while we waited to go into the lab for the lesson.

'We got talking and he made a big impression on me, on everyone actually – he was very handsome, and tall.' She gives a girlish laugh: 'He was the only man I'd ever been able to dance with'.

The young couple had other things in common beyond science and dancing – chiefly, theatre and cinema, both becoming members of the People's Theatre and the Tyneside Film Society. The TFS played a critical role in promoting film culture in the North East for 35 years. Run by volunteers like Heinrich Przibram, the society was the only way enthusiasts could see foreign language and minority interest movies until the Film Theatre opened in 1968, flying the flag for film, film education especially, for a generation. It can't be a coincidence that the British Film Institute chose as the location for only its second regional theatre a city that had such strong traditions, nurtured by people like the Przibrams.

But film wasn't the only thing that brought the couple together. There was also the matter of their names.

'I'd never liked the name Rosamonde – it just didn't seem me – and so I became Rommi and Heinrich became Heini, and that's how we were known from then on. I left college in 1940 – you could only get a grant if you intended to teach and I didn't want that, but I became a test chemist at the Newcastle Gasworks, while Heini went on with his course before various difficulties intervened.'

That is one way of describing summary incarceration. In 1940, after Churchill's infamous instruction to 'collar the lot!', thousands of 'enemy aliens' were locked up, though often with touching British courtesy.

The first Heini knew of his fate was when a policeman knocked on the door of his lodgings and asked if it would be convenient if he returned at 5pm to arrest him. He was interned in Huyton outside Liverpool and then on the Isle of Man, where he mounted entertainments and made friends with Dadaist artist Kurt Schwitters (whose masterpiece *Merz Barn* wall can be found in Newcastle's Hatton Gallery) before it was decided he wasn't a threat to national security and released to return to Newcastle – and Rommi.

'We married in 1943 but because of the regulations of the time, the only way we could do it was by me actually becoming a German citizen. So we began a very happy life together.'

An important part of this life was bound up with films, especially on Sundays, when the Tyneside Film Society met to screen films at the Haymarket. In 1940, cinemas were forced to close on Sundays, but Dixon Scott Junior, who'd taken over the family business, allowed the TFS to use the News Theatre instead. Rommi remembers him being very good to the Society over many years.

In front of me I have a programme for the '64th Exhibition of the Society', held on 9 February 1941, which featured the documentary *Atlantic*, about trade with the US, and the main feature, the 1939 French film *Les Gens du Voyage*, Jacques Feyder's delightfully corny melodrama about circus life. Between these the following records were played: Richard Strauss' *Don Juan* (a surprising choice for 1941), Schubert's *String Quartet in A Minor* and *Gavotte for Sextet* by Thuille. The choices weren't always so high-minded: the feature that ran on the weekend I was born in 1951 was the Marx Brothers' *Monkey Business*.

Throughout the Fifties the society flourished, its membership growing steadily from 600 to 1,600. This meant there had to be overspill screenings at the Tatler at the top of Northumberland Street. The timings were staggered, so that completed reels at the News Theatre could be couriered in a Society official's rucksack up to the Tatler. Only on one occasion was the Tatler screening delayed – during the Festival of Britain of 1951, when the courier's bike was held up by a military parade.

Usually the man who handed over the can of film to the courier was the News Theatre's young projectionist Alan Riding, who has never forgotten Heini's courtesy to him. 'He always came to me after screenings and asked me what I thought of the film. He said he valued my opinion because I'd seen more films than any member of the society. I really appreciated that. My love of French films dates from that time.'

It wasn't until 1962 that the TFS's near 30-year connection with the News Theatre was severed. In that year the People's Theatre Arts Group moved from its tiny theatre in the West End to the cavernous Lyric Cinema in Heaton, which provided the TFS with a more comfortable home. At the age of ten, I saw one of the People's last productions at Rye Hill – a thoroughly terrifying production of *Sweeney Todd*, with Rommi as Mrs Lovett, maker of pies with special ingredients. While she acted, Heini produced short films, often with the Newcastle Amateur Cinematographers' Association.

'Heini was a great prodder – he was very good at getting people to do things', says Rommi. He also had a meticulous attention to detail, essential for a film producer – and was a production engineer for George Angus Ltd. The husband and wife team ran the TFS together for years: he was the chairman, she was the secretary.

Heini also made the Society's 25th anniversary film in 1959. There is a brief shot of him near the end and I freeze-frame the DVD to take a closer look. He is everything Rommi suggested: tall, slender, good-looking – a kind of bespectacled Cary Grant – with an intelligent, thoughtful and slightly quizzical expression on his face. He seems to have left Vienna far behind.

I also like the commentary of the film, which is cool, clear and well-modulated. The voice belongs to the Rommi of 50 years ago.

At the end of our conversation, I ask Rommi what her favourite film is. Without hesitation she answers: 'Marcel Carné's *Les Enfants du Paradis*, because it's a film about a theatre – the two great passions of my life, besides Heini'.

Opposite page:
News Theatre entrance, 1938.

5 | 'It was warm and comfy. There were plenty of tramps'

Above: Jean Murray (left) and friend Hazel at Butlins in Ayr, early 1950s.

Courtesy of Jean Murray

Jean Murray was a country girl, brought up on a farm at Carrick Hill, near the village of Hedley on the Hill, ten miles south west of Newcastle. When she left school in the late 1940s she took a course at Colson's Secretarial College in Wallsend, then got a job at the British Paints factory in Shieldfield in the east end of the city. On Friday afternoons, she finished early, but the bus home didn't leave Marlborough Crescent Bus Station until 5.30pm, so she had time on her hands and like many thousands of other Tynesiders, she found a perfect way of killing it.

'I had my routine on Friday afternoons, a way of celebrating the end of the week. I'd catch a bus into town, go to Woolies in Northumberland Street and have a coffee and one of those chocolate-covered cornflake cakes and then wander down to the News Theatre for an hour or two.'

The decade following the end of the war in 1945 was the heyday of the News Theatre. Audiences remained as high as ever, and as rationing eased, wages rose and life slowly began to get better, more and more people flocked to the Coffee Rooms. A new generation of customers got the News Theatre habit, and it became part of their weekly routine. All of this was excellent news for its owners, the Scott family, in particular managing director Dixon Scott Junior, who came home from war service and ran the cinema with a light and benevolent touch for more than 20 years. The News Theatre was like a little gold mine, and the family obviously believed the lode would never peter out – but it did. New technology – in the form of television – inexorably throttled the life out of it, and Scott was unable, possibly even curiously unwilling, to do anything about it.

The cinema's slow death seemed unimaginable in those first years of peacetime. Jean Murray was part of the new generation of News Theatre patrons. Her memories of her Friday afternoons after the Second World War are evocative, and bring a smile to her face – and mine – as she brings them to mind.

The photos on the stairs of glamorous movie stars, including Margaret Lockwood...

The smoke of a hundred cigarettes caught in the lights of the projectors – and the groans from the audience when the reel snapped and the screen went blank...

The adverts for local shops – Fenwick, Binns, and the school outfitters, Raymond Barnes, where she got her maroon and gold uniform for Colson's College...

The slumped figures of lorry drivers, fast asleep...

Watching the footage of King George VI saying goodbye to his daughter, Princess Elizabeth, at Heathrow as she and the Duke of Edinburgh set off on a world tour in 1952 and thinking how ill he looked – the old King died a few months later...

Her discovery of the Coffee Rooms – and her favourite dish for years to come: kidneys and gravy on toast...

Meeting her future husband Ralph and going on a first date, not at the News Theatre but at the Stoll. She has no memory however of the film...

Jean leans back on her sofa and sighs: 'Halcyon days they were, wonderful times to live in...'

These memories are typical of the surviving customers of the News Theatre of this post-war period 60 years ago. For many people the cinema remained their main access to news and current events. Suzy Varty used to be taken by her cousins as a small child and lapped up the newsreels – the only way she could find out what was happening in the world till a TV appeared in her home when she was 11. It's no exaggeration to say that the News Theatre played a vital role in educating and informing Newcastle's citizens, present and future.

For many others the theatre was simply a place to spend a pleasant hour or two. Courting couples often behaved in uninhibited fashion in the circle's double-seats, thinking they couldn't be seen in the dark, but Ossie Nicholson also remembers the 'cinema pests' who'd sit next to single women and try to chat them up – or worse.

Below: Audiences at screenings mounted by the Tyneside Film Society at the News Theatre in the late 1950s.

Alan Riding, who came to work at the cinema as a 17-year-old projectionist in 1954, remembers a different kind of harassment: he was once groped by a much older usherette. This wasn't his first experience of such hanky-panky – at his previous cinema, the Grainger, one patron was fond of exposing himself by raising a strategically-placed bowler hat on his lap, until the day he was led away by the police.

Cynthia Campbell was first taken by her family as an eight-year-old in the late Forties and soon became a regular. Visits were usually preceded by a pot of winkles at Lilburn's Seafood Shop nearby or an ice-cream from Mark Toney's. The Coffee Rooms were deemed too expensive, but Cynthia soon fell in love with the building:

'It was so exotic at a time when all buildings were black and gloomy, and the people were a bit like that too. We didn't get a paper at home, so I really appreciated the newsreels. It brought things to life in a way that the radio didn't. The commentary was rather patronising – but even as a child you knew you were being sold something.'

Frank Knaggs also remembers the distinctive voices of these commentators – people like Lionel Gamlin, Bob Danvers-Walker and EVH Emmett.

'They were all rather posh, not in an aristocratic way, but rather like Captain Mainwaring in *Dad's Army*. They wouldn't say 'bank' but 'benk'. They were always loud and cheerful, shouting like racing commentators, except when they were talking about the Royal Family, when they went all soft spoken and deferential.'

Bill Campbell went to the News Theatre with two aunts and assorted cousins and the children's favourites were the cartoons – *Tweety Pie, Heckle and Jeckle, Looney Tunes* – and a series of one-reel films with an American comedy act called the The Bowery Boys. His own particular favourite was a series of American trick-photography shorts featuring Joe McDoakes.

Charlie Hall fondly remembers a series of archive films on historic transport assembled by John Huntley, but he and many others were less impressed by an apparently endless series of travelogues made in the US called *FitzPatrick's Traveltalks*, featuring capering chimps, cheerful natives doing exotic things and excruciating commentary by said FitzPatrick intoning over the same final shot, 'And as the sun sinks slowly in the west...'

Left: Newcastle United's Joe Harvey lifting the FA Cup at Wembley following their second victory in 1952.

Rather more popular was the coverage of great sporting events, culminating in Newcastle United's three FA Cup Final victories in three years in the early Fifties. The young Doug Weatherall, later football correspondent for the *Daily Mail*, will always remember seeing the newsreel shot of a Jackie Milburn thunderbolt during an away tie at Portsmouth: 'He turned on the ball and hit an unstoppable shot from about 30 yards – it never rose above knee height – and Butler in the Portsmouth goal had no chance as the ball went to the left of him. It was magnificent, unforgettable.'

Bill and Cynthia Campbell were both Newcastle fans then – before they met – and still are today.

'It seems strange to recall it now, when so much football is on TV, but back then you had to wait from the Saturday of the final to the following Wednesday before you could see what happened. It was agonising,' says Bill.

Not that gratification deferred was necessarily gratification enjoyed, as Cynthia remembers.

'We watched those victories over and over again – everybody did, the place was heaving – but it was very unsatisfying. The footage was so badly filmed and edited. You wouldn't see the build-up to a goal – there'd be a bit of stuff happening in midfield and then they'd cut to the ball in the net and the commentator getting all excited and you thought, is that it?'

Youngsters like Bill and Cynthia were encouraged by the cinema management to join its 'Junior Film Club (Experimental)', which was held in post-war years in the second floor Lecture Hall on Saturdays at 10am and 2.15pm. Organised by the Northern Counties Children's Cinema Council, its programme was a familiar mix of entertainment and education. On Saturday 3 May 1952, when 333 children attended, it included the following:

> 'Trigger Magic – some clever sharp-shooting with a rifle, 10 mins.
> You and Your Rabbit (RSPCA)
> Three Bags Full – Part 3 of Serial
> Interval
> Then full feature We Dive at Dawn – submarine's daring exploits
> in sinking German battleship in Kiel Canal.'

The club published its own weekly magazine, which that Saturday told its members that use of the lift in Newe House was forbidden and printed comments about the previous episode of *Three Bags Full*. These included:

> 'The bad table manners would have an adverse effect on
> young children.
> Super.
> Too stupid for words.
> This film made me feel hungry and sleepy.'

Jack Kennedy became a member of the Film Club in about 1946 after he heard about it from one of his masters at school. He remembers seeing a version of *Emil and the Detectives* and the biopic *Young Tom Edison*, but his lasting memory is of the morning a couple of years later when there was a screening of a Marx Brothers film, probably *A Night at the Opera*.

Below left to right: Junior Film Club (Experimental) magazine programme covers, post-war.

'There was often a speaker of some kind after the film – after *Emil*, it was a French lady – but this morning the man in charge said we had a very special guest and some Marx Brothers music played and on to the stage came – we couldn't believe it – Chico Marx himself, dressed in his usual outfit and his silly hat. It really was him – he and his brothers were appearing at the Empire in Newgate Street – and he was smashing, doing his patter and even sitting down at the piano, and doing the little tricks with his finger we'd all seen so many times on the films. It was just amazing to me – to see a Hollywood star in the flesh at our little Film Club.'

If these first few years after the war were golden times for cinemagoers like Jack Kennedy, they were doubly so for the cinemas themselves. There were dozens of picture houses on Tyneside and with full employment and people hungry for entertainment, pretty much all of them all, elegant or scruffy, were packed out and making money.

As an apprentice engineer at Vickers-Armstrongs in Walker, Charlie Hall couldn't help noticing how many lads at the shipyard used to bunk off to the nearby Gloria, which specialised in westerns, sci-fi and horror flicks. Bill Campbell was a regular at a Wallsend cinema officially called the Royal, but universally known as the Ranch because it too specialised in westerns. Bill laughs at the memory.

'People used to say that if you went in wearing a sweater, when you came out it had turned into a jumper. The Ranch was quite literally a fleapit.'

Not many people realised it yet, but the golden days were almost over. If there was a moment that constituted a turning point, it was probably a wet day in June 1953.

When George VI had been crowned in 1937, Ossie Nicholson and family had taken a bus from their home in Gateshead to watch it in colour at the News Theatre. But this time they travelled to London, not to line the streets by Westminster Abbey, but to watch the coronation of Queen Elizabeth II in black and white – on a friend's television.

Dixon Scott Junior, now in charge of the News Theatre, was also in London that day. He'd taken his own equipment down in a van to shoot the cinema's own version of the greatest of State occasions, but it turned out badly. According to his oldest daughter Bridget, the colours weren't right, and it all looked rather strange.

'He showed the film anyway, but he was so upset. My grandfather and him had always been keen on screening their own footage of big events, but that was the end of movie-making at the News Theatre,' says Bridget.

It is hard not to see in those running colours and a proprietor's disappointment an omen for what was to come. The inexorable rise of television in the next two decades would be the biggest challenge cinema had ever faced. Many theatres would die, some would survive; but there seemed no hope for the news theatres – the new medium increasingly rendered them obsolete. Dixon Scott must have known this – the reason perhaps that he hated TV and for years wouldn't have one in the house – but for one reason or another he failed to act upon it. He didn't sell when he had the chance, but merely hung on to the death. As a result, the remaining 15 years in the life of his father's News Theatre would be a long, drawn-out diminuendo.

Dixon Scott Senior had given his sons everything that his modest beginnings had denied him: education, a very comfortable upbringing and a secure income for life. Dixon Junior went to boarding school in Stratford-upon-Avon and then went into the family business. Two of his daughters believe that he always wanted to be a doctor – as his younger brother Ridley became – but his father wanted him by his side and gave him an apprenticeship in cinema management at the Haymarket. When the News Theatre was finished, Dixon Junior became its manager as well as a director. Dixon Senior clearly wanted someone he could trust; he was also replicating the arrangement at his very first cinema, the Kino in Jarrow, when he'd shared its management with his brother JR, and its running with four other siblings. He was a strong family man. In addition, by 1935 he was increasingly ill with his failing heart. He was simply not up to the task of running his new venture, and after he died suddenly early in 1939, his son was on his own.

Not for long – Herr Hitler saw to that. Dixon Junior went to war and his mother Virgi took control of the News Theatre, helped in its day-to-day running by the morning-suited Mr Storey. Virgi's particular province was the Coffee Rooms.

One could argue that during the war and after managing the cinema consisted largely of counting the money. In 1940 each of the four directors of Haridix Ltd – Virgi and her three sons – were each paid dividends of £8,000, the equivalent of £230,000 at today's rates. (A small portion of company profits came from leasing out the Haymarket and rent from properties nearby, but the bulk came from the News Theatre.) It's likely that the cinema kept generating this level of profit certainly until 1955, when ITV came on air and TV ownership went through the roof. The Scott family was already well-off, but the News Theatre made them very rich.

Dixon Scott Junior came home from war two years after everyone else, in 1947, his battalion of the Northumberland Fusiliers having been kept on in Germany for reconstruction work. He was a burly but elegantly-dressed man who'd been a useful light-heavyweight boxer before the war, when he settled into family life and had his first child, Ann. During leave from his unit, he met his second wife Bridget Atkinson at a dance in the Old Assembly Rooms. It was love at first sight, and family legend suggests they immediately 'eloped' in his sports car to the rather unlikely lovers' hideaway of Belford.

Below: 'It was love at first sight...' Biddy, the soldier's sweetheart.

Bridget, henceforth known as Biddy, was part of a prominent Northumberland family whose various members had been early investigators of the Roman Wall, towed Cleopatra's Needle from the Nile to the Thames and supplied Newcastle with gas. Her brother had started a flying club on a field on the other side of the garden wall of their substantial home. This is now Newcastle Airport. Biddy was willowy, beautiful and sweet-natured. When she first met her Dixon, who bore something of a resemblance to Clark Gable, he was in the Army, and she was in the Wrens, driving ambulances. As soon as they married they commenced to have children, lots of them. It was evidently a love match.

'They were always snogging, kissing and fondling each other,' recalls their youngest daughter Phillipa, known in the family as Philly. 'It was so embarrassing when we were kids, but so very touching to remember now.'

When Dixon Junior finally returned from war service, he found his mother Virgi in charge of the family business, as she had been for the last eight years. Anxious to be his own man, he took over by the not entirely subtle expedient of moving her desk gradually closer to the door and settled down to enjoy the salad days of the cinema.

His daughter Anthea remembers his daily regime:

'After the war we lived in this great rambling house called Shortlands in Graham Park Road in Gosforth that gradually filled up with children, mostly girls. Dad usually avoided family breakfasts and would get up after we went to school, have his own leisurely breakfast, stroll into the cinema, lunch at the Pen and Palette Club and spend much of the afternoon at his beloved library, the Lit and Phil. We didn't see that much of him. He smoked a pipe and got rather large. I loved him dearly, but I can't help thinking Dad was maybe a little lazy. After all he was handed the business on a plate.'

All of the Scott children from his second marriage – and in the end there were seven of them, though two died – got to know the News Theatre well. It was their private playground. Eldest daughter Bridget:

'My sister Susan and I used to be taken to the cinema on Sunday afternoons by our father, probably to get us out from under Mother's feet, while he worked on the films for the coming week, choosing what he wanted to be in the programmes. They had reel-to-reel equipment and it made a lot of clackety buzzing noise back where the projectors were,' adds Rachel. 'Father would shout 'Cut' at the projectionist from the middle of the seats. The seating area was a great place to play hide and seek in the dark, if the films were ever boring.'

It was during these sessions that Dixon became a censor, removing from these innocuous newsreels anything he thought might offend his family audience. His youngest daughter Phillipa:

'I think he didn't want the audience to view anything he wouldn't let his daughters see. He put women on a pedestal. He adored his mother and his wife and always stood up when a lady entered the room. He was very indulgent to us when we were little.'

Anthea used to invite her whole class to her birthday parties held in this upstairs cinema, which was also let out to the Tyneside Film Society, the King's College Film Club and the Indian Welfare Association.

'Dad would let me watch whatever films I liked so we'd always have two hours of *Bugs Bunny*. Waitresses would appear with trays of sandwiches and drinks, then we'd chase each other along the rows and onto the stage, where there was a grand piano. These women were lovely. When I went into the Coffee Rooms, they'd make a great fuss and say, what would you like, poppet? That was always limeade, and I remember opening the bottles on a big opener on the wall. I loved doing that.'

Rachel also remembers taking her friends into the Coffee Rooms and ordering whatever they wanted.

'I think this got a bit much for the restaurant manager. He was tall and sallow, very thin from being a prisoner of war in the Second World War. His name was Mr Hall. I don't think he liked me, as I'd go freely into the kitchen, asking for God knows what for hordes of pals, ice cream sodas mostly. I was unaware of doing anything wrong, but he probably would have thought of the boss's daughter as a spoiled brat.'

In fact Mr Hall held Dixon Junior, if not his daughters, in some awe. He'd been his batman during the war and often saluted him when they met. In the class-permeated 1950s, he was less respectful to the cinema's projectionists who he thought unworthy of being allowed into the Coffee Rooms, even when they were on their days off and accompanied by their wives.

Dixon Junior was less dismissive of these 'other ranks' and seems to have become fond of his youngest projectionist, Alan Riding, for whom he wrote a glowing testimonial when he finally left in 1960, having just married the cinema's booking clerk, Doris.

'Everyone was scared of him – he was a forbidding looking man with a military bearing – but I always tackled him head on. The impetuosity of youth he called it. I loved music and once suggested we should put on some films on the subject. So we put together what he called Opera Week, and the highlight was a biography of the singer Richard Tauber. We had queues round the block all week.'

This kind of initiative seems to have been rare. Naturally there were problems for the cinema's management from time to time, as when a gang of teddy boys slashed the seats, but the News Theatre seems largely to have run itself after the war. This only became a problem when fewer people started coming through the doors.

One of the Coffee Rooms' regular customers in the Fifties was Ossie Nicholson, who met his insurance salesmen colleagues there. Ossie was 'the man from the Pru' in Gateshead and vividly remembers visiting a customer with his supervisor one evening to finalise a policy – and lucrative commission – and being told to come back in an hour as the family were all watching *Dick Barton* on TV. 'It was the coming thing, everyone knew it,' says Ossie.

That must have included Dixon Scott, yet he went on as before, even after some of the newsreel companies on which his cinema depended began to fold, sticking to his daily routine of lunch at the Pen and Palette and then on to the Lit and Phil, apparently shutting his mind to commercial realities.

Above: Tyneside regular and insurance salesman Ossie Nicholson and his wife Phyllis at a Prudential staff dance at the Brighton Ballroom, Newcastle, in 1957.

Courtesy of Ossie Nicholson

His brothers Harry, a publisher living in Henley, and Hexham doctor Ridley, were not so blind. As the other directors of Haridix (following the death of their mother, Virgi), they had increasing concerns about the falling value of the family business and discussed them with their elder brother. In the early Sixties, his daughters believe, he bought out their shares of the business. In 1962, a short time later, at the age of 54, he suffered a severe stroke while playing cricket in the garden with his children Phillipa and Ridley, his wife, and family friends.

Biddy Scott stepped in to help run the business, but relied on the staff a great deal, including the general manager Jack Clitheroe (an ex-projectionist who changed his paper collars twice a day), Coffee Rooms manager Mr Hall and the fearsome-sounding Thompson sisters who ran the kitchen. This wasn't easy for Biddy, but she put a brave face on it, telling her accountant that running the place was cheaper than having a psychiatrist.

'My mother tried but really she was a disaster in business,' says daughter Phillipa. 'She'd been on various committees including one running the Northumberland Show and thought she could cope with the News Theatre, but she couldn't. Some people took advantage. I waitressed there myself for ten years on and off while at school and college and saw it for myself.

'My mother kept it going because she thought Dad might recover and come back to run it. Well, he did a bit, but not very effectively. He wasn't a great businessman. Dad kept it going, but he should have sold it years before.'

When I ask Phillipa why her father didn't do the obvious and sell the business in its heyday, or at least when the spread of TV quickened, she stops to think.

'I think it was a family thing. The theatre had been his father's pride and joy, and he just couldn't bear to let it go, it would have been a betrayal. So he kept it going out of a sense of duty, but after 1955 it all slowly dribbled away. Then it began to lose money and he couldn't sell it, it was too late, everyone knew it was dying.'

In the summer of 1966, a few weeks after England's World Cup triumph, a 16-year-old lad called Ray Reed got the job of apprentice projectionist at the News Theatre. In fact he's still working in the same projection box, having been there most of his working life. His memories of the two years that followed provide a vivid picture of the News Theatre at the fag-end of its life.

'It was well worn and shabby. Amazing really that it was still going – people didn't come to watch the news, but to rest and have a kip. It was warm and comfy. There were plenty of tramps.

'But the projection equipment was modern – Kalee 21's. I was the apprentice, under a chief and second projectionist, but that soon changed. The second was convicted of handling stolen car parts, then the chief – he was always in The Grapes, the pub along the lane, and used to send usherettes for his brown ale, he got the sack for being drunk on the job and having a flaming row with Mr Scott.

'He was a canny bloke. When all the sackings happened I was called into his office and told I was getting a rise, from £3 to £5.'

It was Ray's job to get Dixon's papers in the morning and on Monday afternoons return his books to the Lit and Phil on the understanding that he could quietly take the rest of the afternoon off.

'Mrs Scott was really nice too. Mr Hall, manager of the Coffee Rooms, was canny too, but when he went out for his lunch some of the staff took advantage of him – they were always dipping into the stock in the kitchen.'

Ray looked after the private hires – the film societies, ad agencies screening films for their clients, and on one memorable occasion, a solicitor in a murder case who wanted to watch a western the accused claimed he'd been watching when his wife was murdered. Ray got a £5 tip.

'I knew it wasn't going to last, everybody did. We all knew the end was coming,' he says.

Finally Dixon himself accepted the inevitable and opened discussions with the British Film Institute which was looking for a site in Newcastle for one of their regional film theatres. The BFI took a lease on the cinema, but not the Coffee Rooms, and the News Theatre finally closed in March 1968, 31 years after it opened, when its social purpose was as shiny bright as its matchless decor. Both now were a little tarnished.

But a new era was beginning and Dixon Scott Junior stepped into the shadows, assuming a role as rather reluctant and often disapproving observer. However, Ray Reed didn't hang around.

'The BFI came up to have a look at the old place, two of them, they were a right pair of twats, and I thought, I'm not stopping here, so I didn't.'

In time he would return – but to a very different institution.

THE JOURNAL
NEWCASTLE-UPON-TYNE,
NORTHUMBERLAND

ISSUE DATED 5 JAN 1968

Ever-open cinema

Although the take-over of the News Theatre, Newcastle, as a base for the National Film Theatre in the city is a bridging operation, it will be permanent until the new home is established in Newcastle.

The British Film Institute will be running this theatre on exactly the same lines as the National Film Theatre in London, and, when it opens in March, films will be shown every day of the year except Christmas Day.

These performances will be open to the public although there will also be a membership scheme, and there will be special club performances in the smaller theatre for members only.

A spokesman for the British Film Institute emphasised that the selection of programmes would be made by them, but they would have the co-operation of the Northern Arts Association, Newcastle University and the Tyneside Film Society.

Right: The Journal announces the takeover of the News Theatre by the BFI – and a new kind of cinema – in 1968.

Dixon Scott Junior

'A mad, screaming, catastrophic kind of house...'

It is a slightly curious fact that none of Dixon Scott Junior's eight children now live in the North East, where he and his father built up the family cinema empire.

Two of them – Susan and Mathew – died when they were children, but the rest have scattered far and wide: Phillipa, an international lecturer in 17th century textiles, lives in Cumbria; Ridley, the only surviving son, works as an IT consultant and lives in Hertfordshire; Ann, from her father's first marriage, is in London; Anthea runs a successful garden-design business from her farmhouse in the Vale of Glamorgan, where she cultivates medlar and other exotic fruit trees; the eldest, Bridget, runs a taxi business with her husband in County Donegal; and Rachel lives in North Carolina and paints in the magic realist style, work which she says owes much to her upbringing and family.

I wonder why this is. Anthea offers her own reason.

'I loved them all, but ours was a very tiring house to live in. I can't tell you how glad I was to leave it. At 16 I went to Switzerland to work as a hotel chamber-maid and never really went back again,' she says.

Home was first a large house in Graham Park Road, Gosforth, and then another in Riding Mill with bigger garden and a country feel that Dixon's wife Biddy craved. It was full of treasures.

Bridget remembers a trunk in which her father kept his uniform and military paraphernalia that we 'raided and took out, which made him cross' and also a portrait of the grandfather they never knew. 'It was very good, but he looked rather stern. Mother moved it from the staircase to a box room because she thought it looked as if he was judging her!'

Phillipa and Ridley remember both homes as happy places, but Anthea tends to remember – well, the noise...

'We were quite an argumentative family, at least us girls. All of us were striking-looking, but there were screaming rows, too many hormones, too much sibling rivalry. We were tomboys – climbing trees, doing mad things on a rope swing, whizzing downstairs on tea trays.

While all this was going on, Mum retired to her beautiful garden. Dad stayed away or just blanked it all,' says Anthea.

When the family lived in Gosforth, such was the wealth generated by the News Theatre they had five live-in staff, including a married butler and housekeeper, who lived on the top floor of the house and (in a curious echo of Carol Reed's *The Fallen Idol*) apparently disliked each other intensely. We don't need to rely on the family for a flavour of the household. John Bradshaw, who more or less single-handedly ran the Tyneside in the (literally) dark days of 1975-76, also lived in Riding Mill and often called into 'Westwood' to give Biddy a lift into town. On one occasion he was waiting for her and a pet goat wandered into the living room.

Once Dixon took it into his head to take the children to his beloved Holy Island, and they had the unforgettable experience of travelling through Northumberland in a pony and trap. The last leg of the journey to their overnight destination – across the Causeway as the tide came in – added a final frisson.

As befitted the family's means, the children were privately educated. The older girls went away to a boarding school in Wales, accompanied by their ponies, but the younger ones, Anthea and Phillipa, went to a private day school nearby, Westfield in Gosforth, which didn't then have a particularly high academic reputation. Anthea left Westfield with three O-levels and says it took her many years to get the education she craved. Phillipa, who also became a student later in life, says she learnt only two things at the school – how to write a cheque and how to step modestly from a sports-car.

The older girls sometimes escaped from Graham Park Road and went to stay with their grandmother Virgi in her extraordinary home in the old walls of Newcastle – Plummer Tower in Croft Street, five minutes' walk from the News Theatre. 'A magical little place', according to Rachel, it was full of the oriental antiques collected by her husband. Her first floor bedroom had an elegant curved window facing the sunrise. Here she would sit at her grand piano, her bulldog Bonnie at her feet, and play immaculately for her grand-daughters, all of whom had been given pet-names by her.

'She was very tolerant of us playing havoc, pulling books off shelves and generally going mad while she played patience. She was a very good cook and served us exotic dinners on thick green glass plates,' remembers Bridget.

Sadly, the magic house was indirectly the cause of Virgi's death. One day in the early Fifties, coming down the stone steps once trodden by Royalist troops in the Civil War, she fell and broke her hip. She died not long afterwards, allegedly leaving her Fenwick account in very substantial deficit. Her son Dixon paid this off in full to preserve her reputation.

Her oldest grand-daughter Ann, child of Dixon Junior's first marriage, remembers going to see her on a return visit to Newcastle as a young woman:

'She was wonderful. She smoked cheroots and baked bread. She opened the door in a flowered pinny. There was a framed embroidery near the door that said 'Welcome' in many languages. She showed my friends around. There were arrow slits in walls – one had a cocktail cabinet in it, and when she opened some champagne she said she used to fire arrows at invading Scots through them! She had a very twinkly sense of humour. She was very kind to me and stayed in touch with me even though Father never replied to my letters.'

It is only very recently, ironically through a BBC News interview with her sister Phillipa about the restoration of the cinema once run by her father, that Ann made contact again with her half-sisters and brother – and they learnt of how he had cut her out of his life. From the hills of North Carolina, Rachel offers her perspective of Dixon Junior: 'My father was a strange man. I remember very good and very bad things about him,' she says. Phillipa meanwhile recalls 'a generous man who always dressed elegantly.'

There's an elusiveness about Dixon Junior from a professional as well as a personal point of view – most evident in those long years in which he did nothing to arrest the slow decline of the family business. But then this was a career not of his choosing and his father obviously cast a long shadow. Dixon Senior can't have been an easy act to follow. Then there are his own half-hidden – and difficult – life experiences. As Anthea says, 'Our family attracted catastrophe.'

Two of the couple's children died under tragic circumstances: Mathew, aged two, from an allergic reaction to a diphtheria immunisation, and the beautiful Susan, aged 17, from Hodgkin's lymphoma. According to their other children, Dixon and Biddy couldn't speak to each other of the loss of their son. Biddy told Rachel that if she let herself cry she was afraid she would never stop.

But every so often, after the News Theatre closed for the night, Dixon would summon his general manager Jack Clitheroe and ask him to organise a personal screening in the cinema upstairs, and there he'd sit by himself in the darkness and watch, often more than once, a cine-film sequence of his dead son as a baby.

Alan Riding was a projectionist at the cinema in the 1950s: 'I liked him, but I did think there was something lonely about him.'

There was almost another tragedy when Biddy's nightie caught alight in her bedroom. The family butler (he whose wife detested him) saved her life when he rolled her up in a rug to extinguish the flames. This was almost a double-tragedy: she was seven months' pregnant with Anthea at the time.

Finally, there is the matter of Dixon Junior's white hair, which so astonished his family when he finally returned home from Europe in 1947. Apparently he rarely spoke about his wartime experiences, but the white hair seems eloquent enough. Certain bare facts are known.

He had a long war with the Northumberland Fusiliers, serving in four separate campaigns. He took part in the battle of North Africa, which left him with a permanent aversion to hot climates (the reason the family later went on holidays to the Baltic); the invasion of Italy, where he took part in the brutal battle to take the strategic stronghold of Monte Cassino; the liberation of France and Belgium, where he met a little girl who told him she liked cats and when he inquired why, she said they tasted nice; and finally the subjugation of Nazi Germany, where he helped resettle displaced persons and had perhaps his defining wartime experience, and the possible cause of that white hair. He took part in the clearance of a concentration camp. Family memory suggests it was Belsen, the very place whose horrors made such an unforgettable impression on the customers of his News Theatre back home in Newcastle. But of course they saw it on film – he experienced it for real. It is perhaps not hard to understand why Major Scott so readily accepted the pleasures of a quiet life.

On his return Dixon went on a trip to reacquaint himself with his beloved Northumberland, and perhaps purge his wartime experiences. Typically this nearly ended in disaster. The kayak he was piloting around the Farnes capsized and he had to swim miles to reach the shore. Biddy raised the alarm and rescuers found him by torchlight, lying exhausted on a beach.

Opposite page: Dixon Scott Junior and family in page from family album, clockwise from top left: returning soldier with daughter, young boy with pet dog, two daughters, and family group in early 1950s, Dixon Scott Junior behind mother, Virgi – note his white hair.

Courtesy of the Scott family

After he closed the News Theatre in 1968, Dixon rarely went back. He died in 1982, aged 72. Biddy, the Grace Kelly of her generation, lived on until 2000, making jam and keeping bees, whose hives she'd dump in the back of her car and drive into the hills so they could enjoy the heather.

By then her children had scattered from Tyneside, but all in their different ways have lived up to the unofficial family motto laid down by Dixon Scott Senior: 'You can do anything you like as long as you want it enough.'

And now we are – more or less – done with the remarkable Scott family, whose deeds and stories, triumphs and tragedies, dominate the first half of the history of what became the Tyneside Cinema.

Yet we haven't even touched on one of the children's many great-aunts – Sophie – who according to Rachel 'was a tiny woman who lived for a while in the Canadian Rocky Mountains in a cabin all by herself. She painted beautiful water-colours of the native American Indians. She was not at all afraid of the grizzly bears and they did not bother her, walking right by her. Maybe they smelled that she was a vegan.'

Opposite page: 'Hugs and Kisses', the Swedish film that embarrassed a first night audience – one of the less revealing scenes.

6 | 'What would life be like without the Tyneside?'

On 17 March 1968, the Tyneside Film Theatre (TFT) opened its doors for the first time in the building that until a few weeks before had been Dixon Scott's News Theatre. A new era was beginning.

The leading officers of the British Film Institute (BFI), which was behind the new venture, arrived in force from London and gave the local press the quotes they were looking for.

'The North East has one of the biggest film-going publics in Britain and we are very grateful to have found a home in the city centre,' said the theatre's new manager, Andrew Douglas-Jones.

John Huntley, the BFI's Regional Controller, told reporters, 'Our aim is to present the best of world cinema.'

But it was left to the institute's director, Stanley Reed, to make the boldest claim. 'I think,' he said, 'we can claim to be adding a new dimension to the cultural life of Newcastle and the North East.'

If these were the high-flown ambitions of the BFI, they had, as they say, a funny way of showing it. When the invited audience took their seats that night, the curtain rose not on some venerable art movie, but an obscure 'saucy Swedish sex comedy', intriguingly named *Puss och Kram* (*Hugs and Kisses*). With star Agneta Ekmanner and husband-director Jonas Cornell in the front row of the circle, Newcastle's great-and-good were reportedly not amused, especially when Miss Ekmanner proceeded in one scene to take her clothes off.

Among the audience were Dixon and Biddy Scott and most of their children. The former proprietor, who had once found it necessary to censor *Pathé News* and *Look at Life*, was acutely embarrassed by the film, especially as his 14-year-old daughter Phillipa had to present the fully-clothed Miss Ekmanner with a bouquet afterwards. The brown hessian wallpaper with which the BFI had covered his father's precious decor merely added insult to injury.

But the watching reporters were delighted. The night before the *Evening Chronicle* editorial had welcomed the new venture which 'will be in the vanguard of a campaign to make going to the pictures a cultural event', but now the press had a juicier story, especially when they discovered that the 15-second 'strip sequence' had been cut for its brief London run, but passed by the Newcastle Watch Committee. The following day they tracked down the committee's chairman, Councillor Tom Waters. His comments did not disappoint, nor do they now:

Kinematograph Weekly: March 23, 1968   23

BFI launches its most ambitious project yet

TYNESIDE Film Theatre, the British Film Institute's latest and most ambitious regional project, opened on Sunday with a public premiere of the Swedish film " Puss och Kram " (" Hugs and Kisses ").

Guests of honour were the film's director, Jonas Cornell, and his beautiful wife Agneta Ekmanner who stars in this, his first feature film. They had been flown from Sweden by the Institute to attend the opening at the 400-seater cinema situated in the heart of Newcastle.

Introducing them, Stanley Reed, Director of the Institute, said how pleased he was that the seventeenth regional project was in such an attractive house. He hoped the Tyneside Film Theatre, which is open to the public, would prove a base for the widening interest in good cinema, as well as a centre for young film makers who at present travelled to London in order to make films.

George Singleton, representing the Governors of the BFI, welcomed the guests at

George Singleton, representing the BFI governors, welcomed guests at the reception following the showing of the film.

the reception following the film. Among those present were the Lord Mayor of Newcastle, Alderman Roy Chadwyn, the Postmaster General, Edward Short, Sutton Blackett, Swedish Consul to Newcastle, Dr. C. I. C. Bosanquet, Vice-Chancellor of Newcastle University, Alexander Dunbar, Director of the Northern Arts Association, and many other figures from the city, Newcastle and Durham Universities, the arts and industry.

Jonas Cornell and Agneta Ekmanner delight the capacity audience with their witty and informative appearances before the showing of the film.

LEFT: On Tuesday the Cornells visited the Institute's main offices in Dean Street, and were shown round by Stanley Reed and John Huntley. RIGHT: Agneta Ekmanner and Jonas Cornell arrived at Newcastle airport on Sunday morning. They had flown from Sweden on the Saturday in time for a press reception and a tv appearance.

A full complement of Institute staff were on hand to greet the guests of honour. Left to right: Michael Webb, programme officer for the regional projects, Stanley Reed, Director, Andrew Douglas-Jones, publicity manager for the Tyneside Film Theatre, Miss Ekmanner, Brian Baxter, press officer, Jonas Cornell and John Huntley, regional controller for the BFI.

Left: 'Kinematograph Weekly' announces the BFI's launch of its 'most ambitious project yet', 23 March 1968.

'We thought nothing to it. It was just a young lass taking her scanties off to go to bed. After all, this is a specialist theatre which goes for these arty-crafty films. She drops off her bra and panties and you see a full view of her, that's all. There was no one else with her and it wasn't at all erotic. You could look on it as art, if you like.'

This may all have been knockabout stuff for the press but the choice of *Hugs and Kisses* (its rumoured next appearance in Newcastle was at the city's 'dirty mac' cinema, the Stoll in Westgate Road) was disastrous for the Film Theatre. This avoidably negative PR cemented in the minds of many people for years into the future the idea that the Tyneside was the home of mucky as well as difficult films – and certainly wasn't for them. It was a bad start – and set the tone for the cinema's troubled history over the next ten years.

Tyneside Film Theatre

The best of world cinema

MARCH

Pilgrim Street
OPPOSITE ODEON CINEMA
Newcastle upon Tyne NE1 6QE
Telephone 21506

CINEMA ONE Open to the public

CINEMA TWO The members theatre

CINEMA ONE			Mar.		CINEMA TWO	
EASTERN FILM SOCIETY	3.30	7.00	1 Sun.	7.30	**CIVILISATION**	Silent/PA
FESTIVAL CHOICE	6.00	8.30	2 Mon.	8.00	History Special: **Industrial Revolution**	
Eric Rohmer's	6.00	8.30	3 Tue.	8.00		
MY NIGHT WITH MAUD (A)	6.00	8.30	4 Wed.	8.00	Cocteau's	
Plus	6.00	8.30	5 Thu.	8.00		
MAX ERNST	6.00	8.30	6 Fri.	8.00	**ORPHEE**	
	6.00	8.30	7 Sat.	8.00		
EASTERN FILM SOCIETY	3.30	7.00	8 Sun.	7.30	**THE GENERAL LINE**	Silent/PA
	6.00	8.30	9 Mon.	8.00	Special: **Jenning Anderson and Watkins**	
	6.00	8.30	10 Tue.	8.00		
FESTIVAL CHOICE	6.00	8.30	11 Wed.	8.00	Bergman's	
BOY (A)	6.00	8.30	12 Thu	8.00		
	6.00	8.30	13 Fri.	8.00	**VIRGIN SPRING**	
	6.00	8.30	14 Sat	8.00		

SPECIAL ALL-NIGHT FILM SESSION FOR MEMBERS
SATURDAY 14th UNDERGROUND U.S.A. Doors open 11.00—Start 11.30—Finish 8.30 a.m.

CINEMA ONE				Mar.		CINEMA TWO	
EASTERN FILM SOCIETY		3.30	7.00	15 Sun.	7.30	**L'ATALANTIDE**	Silent/PA
GOSPEL ACCORDING TO		6.00	8.30	16 Mon.	8.00	Sports Special: **CANOEING**	
ST. MATTHEW (U)		6.00	8.30	17 Tue.	8.00		
		6.00	8.30	18 Wed.	8.00	Permissive Society	
Northern Premiere	3.30	6.00	8.30	19 Thu.	8.00		
Cliff Richard in	3.30	6.00	8.30	20 Fri.	8.00	**DANISH BLUE**	
TWO A PENNY (U) 1.00	3.30	6.00	8.30	21 Sat	8.00		
EASTERN FILM SOCIETY		3.30	7.00	22 Sun.	7.30	**NANOOK OF THE NORTH**	Silen /PA
		6.00	8.30	23 Mon.	8.00	Special: **FLYING SCOTSMAN**	
Disney's Fifty		6.00	8.30	24 Tue.	8.00		
Magical years		6.00	8.30	25 Wed.	8.00	Permissive Society	
GREAT LOCOMOTIVE	2.30	6.00	8.30	26 Thu.	8.00		
CHASE (U)	2.30	6.00	8.30	27 Fri.	8.00	**THE NAKED KISS**	
	2.30	6.00	8.30	28 Sat.	8.00		
EASTERN FILM SOCIETY		3.30	7.00	29 Sun.	7.30	**THE SPY**	Silent/PA
Matinees :				30 Mon.	8.00	Sports Special: **FOOTBALL**	
HUGO AND JOSEFIN (U)		Daily at 2.30		31 Tue.	8.00		
				1 Wed.	8.00	Permissive Society	
Evenings :				2 Thu.	8.00	**HERE IS YOUR LIFE**	
WONDERWALL (X)				3 Fri.	8.00		
	Nightly at 6.00	8.30		4 Sat.		**Theatre Open**	

Seats can be reserved for any and all the programmes by calling
at the Box Office (Mon.-Fri. 5-9 p.m. Sat. and Sun. 3-9 p.m.)
or Telephoning Newcastle 21506.

It shouldn't have been like that, for the Tyneside was part of an ambitious plan for cinema outside London. Since the early 1960s the British Film Institute, the publicly funded body promoting film heritage and culture, had been looking for a site in the North East to open a branch of its London flagship, the National Film Theatre. When the TFT opened, Newcastle joined London and Manchester as the only full-time film theatres in the country. By 1971 the BFI had 36 theatres around Britain, but the majority were run part-time and the Tyneside remained one of its most ambitious regional commitments.

From the start its aims were clear: to screen the best of world cinema from all periods and all countries of the world, offering an attractive alternative to commercial cinemas; secondly, to promote the use and appreciation of film; and finally, to encourage local film production.

The programme for the first year, with the exception of *Hugs and Kisses*, squarely met the first aim. There were some outstanding recent releases, including Ingmar Bergman's *Persona* and Robert Bresson's *Mouchette*, and a good number of classic revivals, like *Les Enfants du Paradis*, *Sherlock Jr.,* with Buster Keaton, and the Bette Davis classic *All About Eve*. It was during that opening season that I saw my first film at the TFT, the rather obscure but utterly delightful *La Kermesse Héroïque*, directed by Jacques Feyder in 1935, which described how the ladies of a small Flemish town in the 17th century, abandoned by their terrified menfolk, dealt with an invading Spanish army. They were beguiled – and so was I.

Praise – or indeed blame – for the new cinema's programme couldn't be directed at anyone actually working there, for in those far-off days the BFI adopted a colonial attitude to its up-country outposts: we pay the costs, you watch what we think is good for you. Everything important was decided at head-office. This was to remain a contentious issue for the next ten years, until an increasing volume of local funding and some tough talking gradually brought control of programming closer to home.

The BFI did however take steps to promote its second aim – broadening the use and appreciation of film. In 1970 the TFT was among the originators of the North East Education Film Project, a pioneering programme to use film to support teaching and learning in schools and promote a wider understanding of film culture amongst young people. The same can't be said of their third ambition, to stimulate film production in the region, which as the Seventies wore on was largely left to Northern Arts. The closest the Tyneside got to movie-making was when the rushes for *Get Carter* were screened there for director Mike Hodges during shooting in 1970.

Opposite page: Tyneside Film Theatre poster, 1969.

On one memorable occasion, recalls manager Charlie Picken, Michael Caine was present and halted proceedings to complain that the projector was running slow. When this was disputed, he said the reason he knew was that Carter's characteristic gesture – running a hand through his hair – seemed laboured. He was proven correct.

Unlike the NFT, the Tyneside was open to the public as well as members, or associates as they were called. There were advantages to being an associate – for eight shillings year they enjoyed exclusive use of the smaller 'club' cinema (now the Roxy) as well as associate-only events and a bi-monthly illustrated programme booklet. But the associates-only policy for what eventually became Cinema 2 reinforced the perception of many people on Tyneside that the place was a private club, and 'not for us'. This became a growing concern for successive managements in the Seventies and Eighties.

It probably didn't help that competition appeared nearby. In 1969, 150 yards up the road, the Tatler closed its doors as a news theatre and reopened as the Classic, with a brief to show offbeat new releases: a lengthy run of *Easy Rider* began (I was there), though management felt the need to reassure punters: 'We have had very large audiences for this film at the Classic Piccadilly and personally have found them very charming people and they caused no trouble.'

Below: Charlie Picken
Courtesy of Charlie Picken

As a result of all these factors – and the fact that its interior was tatty and projectors unreliable – the Tyneside lost £15,000 in its first year, though this deficit was wiped out in the second after some staff were made redundant. A new manager arrived in April 1971 – Charlie Picken had run the Film Guild in his native Edinburgh – and his first impressions were mixed. He was charmed to receive a copy of Scott Dobson's *Larn Yersel' Geordie* from his friendly staff, but less impressed when he noticed that the prices shown at the box office two months after decimalisation were still in pounds, shillings and pence.

In time he got to know his landlord. The *Hugs and Kisses* debacle had left Dixon Scott Junior with a profound distrust of the BFI and its staff, but Charlie managed to warm him up with a season of Buster Keaton films with piano accompaniment, which he loved.

'He was always on at me to lift the carpets in the foyer and landings so his father's precious mosaic floors could be seen again. I couldn't do that for him, but he did begin to think that maybe we weren't all bad. He was kind to me and let me have an office upstairs so I could move out of the underground boiler room,' says Charlie.

Meanwhile Picken attempted to wrest programming from the central control of the BFI, but his imaginative initiatives were only permitted at the edges: he began late-night and all-night horror shows – 'the Friday Night Scream-In' – and also screened Tom and Jerry evenings which proved enormously popular with students, though one night a posse of police officers from the station nearby piled in.

There were other new projects: in 1972 a monthly series of talks began called Film-makers Talking, an idea dreamt up by Murray Martin of the Amber film collective. With Northern Arts, the TFT also helped set up a series of mobile screenings in towns and villages in Northumberland and Durham called the Moving Picture Show.

But the cinema was constrained by its branch-office identity. It did have a board of local trustees but according to one of its members, John Bradshaw, it only met twice a year, mostly for pleasant discussions about members' favourite films, details of which were respectfully passed to the panjandrums of the BFI for their lofty consideration.

Above: The 'Shields Weekly News' reports a development in Pilgrim Street, 22 August 1973.

Bradshaw, who was soon to play a major role in the survival of the cinema, first came to Newcastle in 1960 to study for a year at the Institute of Education at King's College. He loved the city but recalls that then its only cultural outposts, at least for him, were the Tyneside Film Society and a coffee bar in Gateshead. Later in the Sixties he returned to the city to lecture at Ponteland College of Education and lived in Bessie Surtees' House on the Quayside, where he shared a staircase with Sandy Dunbar, head of the newly created North-East Arts Association, forerunner of Northern Arts.

'One morning I stopped him on the stairs and asked why the association didn't have a film and photography panel to build up work in that area. So he took me at my word and set one up and I ended up chairing it. Serendipity is a funny thing – if I hadn't gone to live in that wonderful old building my life would maybe have taken a very different course,' says John.

Partly as a result of the growing ambition of Northern Arts and the desire of Tyne Wear County Council to play a role in culture, in 1973 the BFI handed the Tyneside over to local control. It's likely that the Institute's reluctance to bankroll the cinema on its own played a part. After five years of direct control from London, and months of negotiations, a new trust was set up, its members representing Northern Arts, the BFI, Newcastle and Durham universities, Newcastle Polytechnic, the North East Educational Project and seven local authorities. The BFI agreed to pay grants totalling £11,000 in each of the first three years and, at Charlie Picken's urging, £22,000 on improvements, including a new projection box in Cinema 2 and new carpeting, seats and decor in Cinema 1.

'We had a lovely handover lunch at the university,' remembers John Bradshaw, 'and there were optimistic speeches and a warm feeling about the future, but it all unravelled rather quickly. Within two years the place had closed.'

The mid-1970s were not a good time for Newcastle's cinemas. The Pavilion in Westgate Road was one of several that closed for good. The experiment in showing off-beat new releases and cult films at the Classic in Northumberland Street (once the Tatler) didn't last long. It soon became a club featuring sex movies and live striptease, and limped along until 1980 when it closed for good and was demolished. It's now a branch of Barclays Bank, with Pret A Manger on the ground floor.

Even the cinemas that survived had a pervasive smell of death about them. Phillipa Turnbull was working at her grandfather's old cinema, the Haymarket, one night in 1975 when *Jaws* was being screened. At one tense moment the cinema cat bit a woman on the ankle and she ran out screaming. A few years later, Bill and Cynthia Campbell were among a sparse audience watching *One Flew Over the Cuckoo's Nest* when the film stopped abruptly ten minutes from the end and the house lights went up. As the audience quietly left the cinema, a member of staff intimated to the Campbells that the reason for the early finish was that the projectionist wanted to get to the pub before closing time.

At the Tyneside itself, there was an incident that symbolised what seemed the death-throes of cinema in the city. One day in 1973 two men in brown coats arrived and carted away the giant globe spun by generations of children and pored over by the families of servicemen during the dark days of the Second World War, an example of Dixon Scott's desire to use the cinema to educate the public. Cinema staff assumed the men were taking the globe away for repair, but of course it never returned. I wonder if it's still got finger-marks on it...

The crisis that hit the cinema two years later, early in 1975, arrived quickly but had its roots in this slowly-building general malaise affecting the business.

Charlie Picken recalls that in late 1974 and early 1975 business dropped off and the cinema had difficulty meeting budget projections. 'We asked for £5,000 more for the next financial year and this prompted a stand-off between the BFI on one side – we already owed some money to them – and Northern Arts and the county council on the other.'

Audiences were indeed falling: in December 1974 and January 1975, they were running at only 12 per cent of capacity. Spooked by these figures and what they represented, the BFI urged Tyne Wear County Council to increase their contribution to the running of the cinema. At a meeting of the trustees on 29 January 1975, it was reported that the council didn't accept the BFI's proposals for a new tripartite agreement with Northern Arts, though they'd be willing to reconsider the matter in a year. Reading between the lines, it seems likely the council felt the BFI was holding a gun to their heads. In any case the Institute decided that if Tyne Wear wouldn't help, neither could they. This in turn put the cinema's trustees in a difficult position. With audiences falling and debts increasing, they decided at a meeting on 7 February to close the cinema, but in the hope it might reopen at some point in the future. To make matters worse, the trust's chairman, Bob Herrick of Tyne Tees Television, resigned, having had the unpleasant task of sacking the staff, Charlie Picken included.

'It didn't help that the Theatre Royal had its financial problems at the same time, and that was obviously higher profile and higher priority. So I got the push and returned to the commercial sector. I went from art-house films at the Tyneside to the raunchy stuff up Northumberland Street at the old Classic, where one of my duties was to introduce strippers on Wednesday lunchtimes. Such is life.'

Fortunately for the cinema, these outgoings led to an incoming: a new chair, in the slim, bearded form of education lecturer and cinéaste, John Bradshaw. But on the day he took over, after he left for a meeting in London, a second disaster struck. There was a fire in the club cinema. John remembers:

'I only heard about it when I got off the train home. I went to the cinema and it was just awful. The place had survived, but the mess was terrible. Water damage had destroyed the lovely murals on the second floor – *The Canterbury Tales* in the Coffee Rooms and the local scenes in the old Tyne Room. I was in despair. On top of that, I opened a fridge that had been switched off and all the ice cream had turned to a mountain of fungus. The foreman in charge of the workmen came to me and said, look at it this way – the only way is up. He was right. We had to get the cinema open again, one way or another.'

Above: Poster for the Tyneside Filmgoers Group, 1975. Is it a bird? Is it a phoenix rising from the ashes?

John buckled down to his task. He battled with recalcitrant insurers and eventually got new carpets, seats and screen for Cinema 2 and a new screen for Cinema 1. He knew someone in the decorating business who loved film and he agreed to come in and redecorate on a promise of being paid later. He also persuaded architect Peter Yates to put his distinctive mark on Cinema 2. Finally John cleaned out that manky fridge, by himself.

But there were others – many others – who felt as strongly about the Tyneside, and their role was just as important in keeping it alive. Audiences may have been small but they were passionate in their support and angered by the closure – devastated, according to one of them, a community worker in the West End called Judith Green.

'People were very upset. There was a protest meeting in the cinema itself, which led to the forming of the Tyneside Filmgoers Group, followed by smaller meetings in the back rooms of pubs, then we held a series of screenings in the cinema to show that there was a real demand for the cinema,' says Judith. These screenings were held on four consecutive Fridays in May-June 1975, publicised by samizdat-style posters advertising some impressive double bills: a meaty mix of *Spirit of the Beehive, Fear Eats the Soul, Some Like It Hot, Once Upon A Time in the West* and others. Tickets were 50p. There were queues outside the cinema, which was packed for every performance, and a petition gathered 4,000 signatures. The group, which had at its core a mix of community activists and academics, then published a cogent case for reopening the cinema. One of its authors was Howard Wollman, treasurer of the campaign and then a sociology research assistant at Sunderland Poly.

'It's just about the only political campaign I've ever been involved with that really worked. Heady days! I still get the occasional reminder of it all when I go through my old papers and discover the odd cheque for 50p,' says Howard, who later moved to Edinburgh.

The campaign was certainly helpful to John Bradshaw – and he tried to assist in a small way. He remembers pushing a trolley through the streets to the Central Station to collect cans of film for the protest screenings.

Meanwhile he was touring the three funders and gradually warming them to the idea of reopening, with, as it ironically turned out, a higher level of subsidy than before: £11,500 from the BFI, £6,000 from Northern Arts and £3,000 from Tyne and Wear County Council. In addition, most of the cinema's debts were cleared and those faithful decorators could at last be paid.

No wonder Judith Green celebrated:

'The cinema survived and thrived. Thank God we did what we did. What would life be like without the Tyneside?'

But at the same time John Bradshaw knew that the running of the cinema had to be fundamentally changed – or it would soon get into trouble again.

'I realised we had to find someone prepared to take on the job of director, not manager, someone who could programme the two screens effectively and imaginatively as well as manage the building and staff,' he says.

T.F.T. Filmgoers Group
INTERNATIONAL CINEMA SEASON at the Tyneside Film Theatre

TICKETS
50p each or
£1.40 for the season
FROM:
Ticket Centre, Saville Row or
199, Hugh Gardens, Newcastle
Tel. 36221 or
at the door

1 FRIDAY MAY 16 7:00 PM
Erice's
SPIRIT OF THE BEEHIVE
SPAIN 1973   CERT AA
Borowczyk's
BLANCHE
FRANCE 1971   CERT AA

3 FRIDAY MAY 30 7:00 PM
Fassbinder's
FEAR EATS THE SOUL
W. GERMANY 1973   CERT A
Louis Malle's
PHANTOM INDIA
FRANCE/INDIA   CERT A

2 FRIDAY MAY 23 7:00 PM
Bogart in Huston's
TREASURE OF THE SIERRA MADRE
USA 1947   CERT A
Monroe, Curtis, Lemon in Wilder's
SOME LIKE IT HOT
USA 1959   CERT A

4 FRIDAY JUNE 6 7:00 PM
Leone's Classic Italian Western
ONCE UPON A TIME IN THE WEST
ITALY 1968   CERT A
Don Siegal's
TWO MULES FOR SISTER SARAH
USA 1972   CERT X

Above: Tyneside regulars flocked to see these films – and helped save their favourite cinema.

Charlie Picken applied but didn't get it – as he wryly acknowledges 35 years later, he talked the language of commercial, not art-house, cinema. In truth John had already made his choice: a woman he'd met at a regional cinema conference in Kendal (he can still remember the sun glinting on Cross Fell as he drove there). Her name was Nina Hibbin.

'She was working as film and photography officer for Yorkshire Arts, but years before I'd read her film reviews which I'd liked – and I liked her too. I told her about the cinema and when the job came up, it wasn't advertised and I told the board of trustees they could meet but not interview her.' He smiles. 'You'd never get away with that now – there were no equal opportunity procedures or anything – but we got absolutely the right person.'

The main reason for this was that Nina immediately grasped that the future of the cinema depended on it reaching out beyond the small hard-core audience that had worked so hard to save it. A much broader group of Tynesiders had to be persuaded that the cinema had something to offer them too. She wanted to occupy the cinematic centre-ground. In this respect it was helpful that her personal taste in cinema was so eclectic. She may have been passionate about East European cinema, but she also adored the Carry On films, and programmed a season of them for the cinema's reopening in May 1976, accompanied by sessions to diagnose their cultural and social significance. That gala week also featured *The Gentleman Tramp*, a new compilation of Chaplin films, accompanied by various classic Laurel and Hardy two-reelers. Injecting some highbrow weight were a Pasolini retrospective and a season of films on 'West Germany Today', headlined by the new Werner Herzog release, *Aguirre, Wrath of God*. There was a new name too – the Tyneside Cinema – to replace the somewhat more elitist sounding Tyneside Film Theatre.

Less happily, the cinema reopened with Dixon Scott Senior's Persian colour scheme in the foyer, landings and on the stairs painted over and lost, happily not for ever. It reappeared on another reopening – in May 2008.

Max Roberts, artistic director of Live Theatre, arrived to study drama on Tyneside around this time and soon discovered the cinema's late night screenings of black and white classics at the weekend:

'I went along and just fell in love with the place – the decor, the sound of the old curtains opening, just the feel of it. Seeing those old films up there on the big silver screen was such a cool idea – it felt like you were watching them in exactly the right context. Remember this was pre-Betamax, never mind DVDs and iPads. You just never got to see these movies except on the telly at Christmas.

'Three from that inspired piece of programming stand out: *Casablanca*, *Some Like It Hot* and *Battleship Potemkin*. I'd never seen the first two on anything other than a small black and white telly so to see them on the big screen was truly inspiring. As for the Eisenstein classic it was a remarkable discovery: I'd never seen anything like it. In some way all three films were important components of my formulating 'sensibility'. I didn't know it at the time but 30-odd years later I can understand why I recall them so vividly. First and foremost they're three of the greatest movies ever made, but accessible and populist in form, all with their roots in middle European Jewish culture, and all of them had something serious to say about the world. Also, they were all in their different ways politically radical. They were everything I like about art and in some strange way symbolic of everything I've tried to create as an artist working in my particular discipline of theatre.'

Some screenings, however, didn't work out quite so well. In the autumn of 1976 a smallish audience turned out to watch the Dick Richards western *The Culpepper Cattle Co.* and found themselves watching *C.C. and Company*, a film about outlaw bikers. In her regular – and sometimes spiky – newsletters to associate members, Nina Hibbin apologised for this error of the distributors, who also often sent the Tyneside lousy prints. She encouraged regulars to offer ideas on programming – there was a suggestion box in the cinema – and welcomed the idea of a Polanski retrospective. A season of the Bob Hope-Bing Crosby *Road...* movies was less warmly received: 'Oh well, if you insist,' she wrote.

At the end of that first season, the local newspaper critics gave their verdict: in the *Journal*, David Durman decried Hibbin's populist touch in screening films that could be found in commercial cinemas, while his colleague Phil Penfold on the *Evening Chronicle* wryly suggested that the cinema might have more success if its programming went beyond what he called 'films about tractor collectives in the Ukraine'. Perhaps then Nina might have reflected that she was getting her programming policy about right.

Later directors of the cinema plotted a similar course and discovered that as a result you can't please all of the people all of the time. Mark Dobson, the current chief executive, wryly notes that he is sometimes teased about 'my radical strategy of putting on films that people actually want to see'.

Hibbin's approach did get her into trouble with the cinematic guardians of the BFI. Fiercely independent by nature, never reluctant to speak her mind, she didn't always want to screen films they wanted her to screen, and they in turn often disapproved of the films she wanted them to book for her cinema. There was also a financial element to the dispute: the BFI had been programming the Tyneside and other regional theatres for years and the more they were able to amortise the costs of acquiring films over various cinemas the cheaper it would be for everyone, especially their flagship National Film Theatre. Eventually there was an impasse, which coincided with the visit to Newcastle of the BFI's new chairman, former Labour politician and *Face to Face* interviewer, John Freeman. All went swimmingly until tea-time, at which point John Bradshaw told his visitor that the BFI was in breach of contract – for failing to hire the films the Tyneside wanted – and that he was considering suing.

There was a sudden chill. Freeman asked searching questions about the background to the row and Nina didn't hold back. Freeman considered – and decided, dispatching an assistant to phone London with instructions to do what the Tyneside wanted.

Not that she always got her way. Like others before her, she felt that the existence of an 'associates-only' cinema upstairs was part of the reason why the public felt the cinema wasn't for them. She felt it was undemocratic and wanted therefore to abolish membership, so that anyone could walk in and see any of the films on show. There may also have been a personal element to the mutual dislike that grew up between her and the Tyneside Filmgoers Group, who were, in Judith Green's graphic phrase, 'mostly Trots and anarchists, while Nina was a hardline old Stalinist'.

Chris Hurt was a member of the group, though without either political affiliation, and a trustee elected to represent the TFG's interests: 'There was immediate and lasting acrimony between Nina and the TFG. Her ambitions were different from theirs. Some of our people behaved badly in meetings. They wanted the cinema run for their benefit – they'd saved it, after all – whereas she wanted to open it up for everyone.'

Nina took her proposal to abolish membership to the board of trustees, which was split 50-50. As chairman, John Bradshaw felt it was only right to use his casting vote to support the status quo. As a result Hibbin didn't speak to him for two weeks, but the rift was soon healed. With her husband Eric as treasurer and secretary, the three made an effective team.

Above: Cinema trustee Chris Hurt.

At the end of the first full year, in the cinema's annual report in May 1977, Nina succinctly described her strategy: 'The main aim in the first full year of operation was to break down the cinema's esoteric image and establish it as a public amenity, catering for all sections of the community.' The long hot summer of 1976 made life difficult but by the autumn the new approach was beginning to work: 'By judicious double programming – one film for the 'fans' and another for the 'buffs' in a combination that created its own special flavour – we were able to draw audiences together from widely differing sections of the population'.

The following year Hibbin started a sponsorship scheme in which clubs and societies worked with the cinema to programme and promote films of interest to them and the general public.

These bodies included the Social Work Film Group, the Science Fiction Film Group, the Architects and Designers Film Group, the North-East Sub-Aqua Society, the Association of Teachers of Spanish and Portuguese and the Elvis Presley Fan Club, whose screenings were always packed. She took delight in pointing out that when *Winstanley*, Kevin Brownlow's film about the Levellers, was screened for members, only 40 people came, but after she did a sponsorship deal with a Civil War re-enactment society, the 150-seat Cinema 2 was sold out.

She also made it possible for individuals to hire Cinema 2 for private screenings. When I left the news-room of the *Journal* in 1977 to take a job in London, I screened the Marx Brothers' *A Night at the Opera* (a film making its third appearance in these pages) for friends and colleagues one Friday afternoon before we all went on the razzle.

All of these initiatives during Hibbin's tenure led to ever-increasing monthly returns. Box office receipts greatly exceeded budget expectations, though there were some increasing costs, for overdue repairs and the paying-off of long-standing debts. But essentially the cinema was working, dragged back from the abyss by John Bradshaw's quiet effectiveness and the force of Nina Hibbin's considerable personality.

Below: The Tyneside foyer gets a period makeover in the 1970s.

As an individual, certainly as an adversary, Nina had what could be called a gamey flavour. For instance, she took a dislike to Biddy Scott, who was still running the Coffee Rooms, possibly on class grounds. Biddy's daughter Phillipa, by now a student, was still waitressing in the café: 'I'm afraid to say she was rather horrible to my mother and me. She wouldn't let me have my grandfather's poetry books, which had been left in the offices, and told my mother she should give all our money to the poor – not that there was much of it left.'

In fact the Coffee Rooms closed – for the time being – in 1978, and an exhibition centre and snack bar opened in its place, the first stage in an ambitious plan to open a film and TV centre where people could attend seminars and courses.

But Nina left this and many other initiatives to her successors. Her husband Eric was increasingly unwell and in 1979 they decided to retire to their beloved North Yorkshire coast. Nina had only been director of the cinema for three years, but they'd been a critical three years, and 30 years later those who worked with her have not forgotten her qualities.

'Nina was determined, far-sighted and tough, in fact one of the toughest people I ever encountered. She had a real vision for the cinema and worked tremendously hard to deliver it,' says John Bradshaw.

Peter Ferres, the BFI's representative on the trustees, believes she was the best thing that ever happened to the cinema. 'If she hadn't come along at that time, when the cinema was so fragile, if she hadn't pushed that populist approach, the cinema would possibly not exist today.'

Finally, there are the words of projectionist Ray Reed, who returned to the cinema after eight years when Nina Hibbin offered him a job over a cup of tea in the Coffee Rooms.

'We found we had things in common. She was a communist and I read the *Morning Star*. We went drinking together – there was no them-and-us with her. She smoked roll-ups with very strong tobacco. She was up-front and extrovert, knew what she wanted – she didn't piss about. Eric was the opposite – so laid back, he almost fell over. They bought a house in Shieldfield and got me to do the rewiring. They liked parties – we had some good times there.

'She was a tough old bitch, but straight as a die. I liked her.'

Peter Yates

'The song is over but the chords go on vibrating...'

The Tyneside is a small temple of the visual arts.

Dixon Scott's architectural vision – Persian detailing on an art deco design – provides a sumptuous frame for the moving images onscreen. But in a corner of the Electra, barely noticed by many, there's a piece of art that belongs to a wholly different tradition, a remembrance of a remarkable artist and architect who cherished the building and made his mark upon it.

In the autumn and winter of 1975-76, Peter Yates worked by himself in the then Cinema 2, which had been ravaged by fire a few months before. The insurance policy paid for new screen, seats and carpet, but there was nothing much left for the decor. In one of various inspired interventions, the cinema's chair, John Bradshaw, invited the architect to refashion the space as he saw fit.

The cinema's walls and ceilings had already been painted by those film-buff decorators, but Yates erected scaffolding towers to over-paint the ceiling in a swirl of amorphous shapes, a style possibly based on a cinema in Strasbourg which Yates apparently admired – it had been designed by one of his artistic heroes, the painter Piet Mondrian.

For several months Yates would turn up at the cinema after work for his regular night shift. John would hand over the keys to the building as Peter often worked very late. Biddy Scott, still running the Coffee Rooms, recalled that he liked music while he worked, and usually wore slippers with odd socks. It was a big job for one man, but Yates did it, before moving on to a stunningly original signature piece – *Lights and Shadows on the Wall*, a reflection of the history of cinema, combining drawings, photomontage (featuring movie greats like WC Fields, Marilyn Monroe and Laurel and Hardy) and a sly wit, as an example of which he incorporated a recessed fire hose into the piece.

But who exactly was the man in slippers?

Peter Yates was born in Essex in 1920, and went to work as a commercial artist in Fleet Street, while beginning his architectural education. During the Blitz he was a firewatcher on the roof of St Paul's, using rowing-boat

oars to flick incendiary bombs onto the street below. On quiet nights he painted moody watercolours of Wren's masterpiece. He then joined the RAF, studied radio engineering at the Science Museum, and was among the first Allied troops to arrive in Paris, where he helped set a transmitting station in the Palace of Versailles.

The months that followed shaped his life. Prepare to be amazed...

One day he was exploring a Parisian side-street and saw a plaque by a door. It read: G. Braque. He knocked on the door, was bidden to enter and found a man working at a desk. They fell into conversation, then a pupil-master arrangement. Thus Yates came to be taught drawing by one of the pioneers of cubism. (Both Braque and Picasso adored the early cinema, were inspired by its French pioneers Méliès and the Lumière brothers, and some art critics – and Martin Scorsese – have suggested that cubism was an artistic response to the moving image.)

Yates also sought out the studio of one of his architectural heroes. He found him rather hungry and dishevelled. Peter Yates offered food, but the Frenchman placed a higher value on the subsequent meeting of minds. He gave the young Englishman a painting, which he signed 'Amicalement, Le Corbusier'.

Yates later recounted his first meeting with the founding father of the modernist movement, who became his lifelong friend, nicknamed 'Corbu':

'Le Corbusier apologised. "See how we are under the Germans" – his dark brown leather jacket looked completely worn out. His had thick wooden soles like sabots with uppers of straw basketwork, and lined with cat fur...

"Can we see your paintings?" He came out of his chair like an eagle and his eyes shone. "You like painting? You are a painter yourself?" And round that marvellous room he went, full of excitement, pouring armfuls of drawings onto the low tables: drawings of stone and women and flowers and fish and fir cones...'

Yates immersed himself in the intellectual life of wartime Paris, meeting people like Gertrude Stein, Alice B Toklas and Juliette Gréco, but eventually returned home and worked as an architectural draughtsman with the Newcastle-born engineer Ove Arup, meeting the émigré Russian modernist architect Berthold Lubetkin, who subsequently asked Yates to work with him on a new town project in a place called Peterlee. So Yates came to the North East – and never left...

Opposite page:
Peter Yates self-portrait, 1940.

Courtesy of Jolyon Yates

Here my own story intersects briefly with Yates's. In the mid-1980s I made a short film about the restoration of a jewel in Lubetkin's canon: the Penguin Pool at London Zoo, with its swirling, swooping concrete ramps over blue-tiled enclosure. I travelled to the old man's cramped flat in Bristol and gradually enticed him from his shell, a process much aided when he learnt I'd been born a few miles from Peterlee. His observations enriched the film, and the few days I spent editing it, cutting together images of man's design, water and penguins at play to the aquarium passage of Saint-Saëns' *Carnival of the Animals*, were among my happiest as a documentary maker.

In the end the three years Yates spent with Lubetkin in Peterlee came to little, but he did meet a kindred spirit in fellow-architect Gordon Ryder, and in the early Fifties they set up their own architectural practice – Ryder and Yates – in Newcastle, which flourished, establishing an unrivalled reputation for innovation in the Modernist style. I read the long list of their commissions and realised I'd been looking at their buildings most of my life: the North Kenton estate, tumbling down a hill on the edge of Newcastle; the thrusting towers of the Northern Gas Engineering Building in Killingworth, the welcoming arms of the Salvation Army Hostel near the Quayside...

In the course of their 30-year partnership, the two men had opportunities to move to London, but stayed put. Ryder loved to sail and built himself a house in Riding Mill near Dixon Scott Junior's, while Yates indulged his passion for painting – ravishing, witty and totally modern depictions of the places he loved, executed with a sharp eye for form and colour – and the Tyneside Cinema.

So next time you're in the Electra look at his gift to the place, recently rediscovered and restored (for which much credit must go to Cyril Winskell, conservation architect for the Tyneside during its recent renovation).

When Peter Yates died in 1982, a young 62, his mentor Lubetkin wrote:

'From the vision
Of his beloved Durham locked in the mists of time to the
Ultramarine rhapsody of Cyclopic islands.
By staking claims on the distance he excites the imagination.
Simplicity, directness and purity gave his work the power.
That was my friend the poet architect.
The song is over but the chords go on vibrating.'

Nina Hibbin

'Steady, no panicking!'

Nina Hibbin only spent three years at the Tyneside Cinema – she was its director from 1976 to 1979 – but they were a critical three years for the cinema, and for her the culmination of a singular career in film, and an even more singular life.

Born in 1922 to parents who'd fled the post-revolutionary turmoil of the Soviet Union, exchanging the poverty of Vilnius for a corner shop in Romford, Nina Masel did a bit of fleeing herself when she was 16, leaving home to escape a domineering mother and settling in Stepney in the East End. Here she found unlikely employment (along with Northumbrian poet Kathleen Raine) as one of the first female correspondents of Mass Observation, the social research organisation set up in 1937 by anthropologist Tom Harrisson, film-maker Humphrey Jennings and poet Charles Madge. Based on an idea bird watcher Harrisson had after leading a nationwide volunteer census of the great crested grebe, Mass Observation recorded everyday life in Britain through a panel of 500 observers who maintained diaries based on recorded conversations at work, home, on the street and in the pub.

Despite her youth, Nina soon proved the most vivid of diarists, even earning herself a wage for her work, with a telling eye for detail, especially behaviour that contradicted the received wisdom of 'Britain can take it'. In September 1939, aged 17, she commented wryly on the scene in her parents' home the Sunday morning war broke out and air raid sirens sounded for the first time, her mother screaming at her to stop playing the piano, her brother and sister wailing in terror and her father issuing peremptory commands reminiscent of Corporal Jones from *Dad's Army*: 'All get your gas masks! Steady, no panicking! Every man for himself!'

Later in the war she worked for *Picture Post,* captioning photographs, before joining the Women's Auxiliary Air Force and being posted to RAF Digby in Lincolnshire, home to a squadron of the Royal Canadian Air Force. Her first impressions of life on an air base would not be found in *Battle of Britain* and countless other war movies:

'Already during the three days I have been here, I have heard that one squadron was sacked in its entirety because 15 of the men caused 15 girls to be pregnant.

That a dance which used to be held in the village hall every week was stopped because there was too much drunkenness, and because several airmen and airwomen were found in bed together, the morning after... The camp dances are simply excuses to get drunk and to find a girl or man.'

After the war, Nina trained as a teacher at Dartington Hall in Devon and then worked at the village primary school in Delabole in Cornwall. Here she failed to keep her longstanding communist convictions to herself, prompting a question in the House of Commons about the subversive activities of certain teachers in the West Country, but her popularity saved her job. Not long afterwards she returned to London and on a demonstration met her husband Eric Hibbin, another free spirit who'd run away from home, in his case to go to sea at 14. He was an organiser for the Communist Party in East London and after they married, Nina combined her teaching career with the job of film reviewer for the party paper *The Daily Worker* (later renamed *The Morning Star*).

Guardian critic Derek Malcolm remembered her arriving for screenings on a motorbike, and the curious fact that she also wrote reviews for the magazine for gentlewomen, *The Lady*. Her reviews remained much the same for both – full of sympathy for working people and against what she saw as the soul-destroying glibness of Hollywood. She was a trenchant critic and pulled no punches, especially when it came to movies she thought revelled in macho posturing. Of Michael Powell's *Peeping Tom,* she wrote: 'From its slumbering, mildly salacious beginnings to its appallingly masochistic and depraved climax, it is wholly evil.' She was almost as unimpressed with a film shot in the city where she was soon to live and work, Mike Hodges' *Get Carter*: 'With confidence, cynicism and considerable skill, Hodges plays upon all those complex and suspect elements which go to make up the English tough-guy image. He has made a film which is rather sick.'

During Nina's decade as a film critic she was a passionate advocate of East European cinema, and a fierce campaigner to persuade British distributors to screen films she believed in, including Ken Loach's now classic *Kes* and many examples of what was then called third-world cinema. For these things alone, Derek Malcolm believes she deserves a place in the history of post-war British cinema. But Nina Hibbin wasn't finished yet.

Opposite page: Film critic Nina Hibbin at press screening for 'Summer Holiday' with members of The Shadows, including Newcastle's own Hank Marvin, far left, 1963.

Courtesy of Sally Hibbin

When her daughter Sally – now an independent film producer – went to university, Nina bolted again, leaving London for Bradford, where she worked as film officer for Yorkshire Arts, giving grants to film-makers for the first time. It was while doing this job that she went to a conference in the Lake District about regional film theatres and there met a man called John Bradshaw, which led to an offer of a job in Newcastle, where she reopened the Tyneside and put it on its feet.

Eric worked alongside her, as finance officer and company secretary (by this stage, says daughter Sally, 'he was virtually unemployable elsewhere'), but when his health began to fail, they retired to a tiny cottage in Staithes in North Yorkshire, then a cottage at Boulby on the Cleveland Way, where before she died in 2004 at 81, Nina edited volumes of poetry by local people, campaigned against the British National Party and opened a café for walkers.

It is said the tea was cheap but the conversation animated and spicy.

Opposite page: Service with a smile – Jackie Turnball in the box office, 1980s.

'I could be flippant and say it almost broke my heart, but really I loved the old place'

Amid the sometime sound and fury of Nina Hibbin's period as director of the Tyneside Cinema, a smaller, quieter revolution was taking place.

The staff of the cinema remained small – in 1979 numbering only six working full-time – but Nina made it her business to appoint a growing number of committed, well-educated young women, among them a recent graduate called Maggi Hurt.

'She more or less took me straight from university. We had a conversation, rather than an interview, and decided we could work together, so she gave me a short contract setting up a film information service, which was used a great deal by students at the poly and the university at a time when film studies were just beginning. This included preparing typed sheets of introduction to films being screened that were available to members of the audience.

'Other women like me were being taken on then, people like Tricia Gillespie and Linda Ramsey. Nina had a flat management structure so you always dealt with her and though she had strong views, she was always interested in your point of view. We all worked very hard – and scrubbed floors when we had to.'

If this kind of commitment from its staff (and customers) had been critical to the survival of the Tyneside Cinema in the previous decade, it was a central part of its thriving in the 1980s. Buoyed by strong creative management and a new strand of art-house cinema aimed at the young, the cinema got through the difficult years of the Conservative Government's squeeze on public spending in the early Eighties and then

Right: Maggi Hurt, who joined the Tyneside straight from university in 1979.

began positively to flourish. Perhaps the most visible feature of this trend was the growing popularity of its festivals, which acquired a national and then international reputation. As ever, this was down to the cinema's happy – and enduring – knack of finding the right people at the right time to manage its affairs.

When Hibbin decided to retire with her husband, she played an important role in making sure her successor was also a woman, backing the application from a 43-year-old Londoner called Sheila Whitaker – and in the process influencing a shift towards new priorities in the decade about to begin.

Sheila Whitaker had previously programmed films at Warwick Arts Centre while studying comparative literature as a mature student at the university. But she'd also spent six years transforming the BFI's archive into a hugely expanded collection of films and photos. The Tyneside job was a big step up: she worked alongside Nina Hibbin for two weeks and was then thrown into the deep end. She wasn't the only one: Margaret Thatcher had just been elected Prime Minister.

Like others before and after her, Sheila soon discovered that at the heart of her new job was the black art of programming. She continued Hibbin's approach, again fighting off the attentions of the BFI officials who wanted to do her job for her, perhaps easing the foot slightly off the populist pedal, with a mix of art-house first runs and Hollywood second runs. She also enjoyed putting together seasons: at first these focused on screen icons – Chaplin and Hepburn, for instance – but gradually turned into rather more imaginative thematic seasons on the French New

Left: Tricia Gillespie, another of Nina Hibbin's appointments.

Wave, Black-American and Nicaraguan cinema, the Urban Nightmare, a Hollywood musical season called Steppin' Out, a series of films focusing on controversial women called Putting the Blame on Mame (after the song in the Rita Hayworth movie *Gilda*) and closer to home, a season of films about mining and shipyards.

But it was with festivals that Whitaker made her mark. The annual Newcastle Film Festival turned into the Newcastle Independent Film Festival that in turn spawned the Newcastle International Independent Film Festival, attracting the best new releases in the non-commercial sector and the most high profile of stars.

In fact festivals had been held at the Tyneside on and off since 1969. The second in 1970 featured a season of films on the theme of revolution, featuring especially the 'new American revolution' and its sundry aspects, including free love, flower power, black power, sex and violence, drugs and censorship. The local press labelled the programme 'trash', which may or may not have been a selling point for its young audience. Nina Hibbin had revived the festival tradition in 1978, but Sheila Whitaker gave it a much higher priority and profile.

Below: Sheila Whitaker, Tyneside director in the 1980s, made her mark with increasingly high profile film festivals.

Many iconic films of the 1980s had their regional or in some cases national premieres at these festivals, among them *Gregory's Girl, My Beautiful Laundrette, Betrayal, Fitzcarraldo,* and *Wise Blood.* Many of the stars or directors of these films came to Newcastle to talk about their films, often interviewed by the *Evening Chronicle*'s Phil Penfold:

'I remember taking Daniel Day-Lewis to the Duke of Wellington in High Bridge to talk to him for an hour about *Laundrette* before interviewing him again on stage. He was delightful. Another time I interviewed Charlton Heston who was appearing at the Theatre Royal in *A Man for All Seasons* and I remember Shelagh McGouran, the Tyneside's PR, telling me, for God's sake don't ask him about guns or abortion. I didn't, but there was a demo against him outside and he had to be smuggled out.'

In 1983 John Hurt came to the festival with a new film version of *1984.* His namesake Chris, a cinema trustee, took his copy of the George Orwell book and asked John to sign it, which he did, inscribing it, 'From one wound to another.'

Many of these festival films were publicised with striking posters, designed by Rob Barnes. He'd been taken on as an inquiry assistant, welcoming people into the cinema as part of a Manpower Services Commission scheme.

One day Sheila Whitaker saw him doodling on a pad. She asked him to work on a leaflet, and from there he graduated to posters.

'I loved it. I learnt graphic design on the job with a lot of help and encouragement from Sheila. The posters were popular and so many people asked for them that she twigged and we started selling them. You weren't a proper student round here in the Eighties if you didn't have a Tyneside poster on your wall. Sheila was brilliant – took the place by the scruff of the neck and dragged it up. It was an exciting place to work – very long hours, but I loved it.'

Sheila Whitaker's most particular memory is of a little known Argentinian film, María Luisa Bemberg's *Señora de Nadie*, which she wanted to screen during the Falklands War. Elaborate arrangements were made in secret to avoid a government import ban by bringing the film from the Berlin International Film Festival, but it eventually arrived at Newcastle Airport in a battered suitcase from New York shortly before it was due to close the event.

But by consensus the most stirring festival event was an all-day screening of Abel Gance's silent epic *Napoleon* at the ABC Haymarket, with a special score played by the Northern Sinfonia, conducted by Alan Fearon. The cinema was packed. Its builder Dixon Scott would have been proud. Not for nothing did Sheila Whitaker claim proudly that there was 'a real cinephile audience in Newcastle'.

Attendances at the Tyneside itself grew during the Whitaker years, after an alarming initial dip, from 83,000 in 1980 to 105,000 in 1984. Despite this, money worries didn't disappear and in April 1982 Northern Arts director David Dougan expressed worries to his colleagues about accumulated debts of nearly £50,000, a likely deficit of £10,000 the following year and the danger of another closure. Yet, in the end Northern Arts took the extraordinary step of making the cinema 'its number one priority at a time when many other organisations were in trouble, for the following reasons: the cinema has 100,000 visitors, an admirable social mix, a wide-ranging artistic programme, strong management and excellent publicity, and one of the few facilities we support that's open every day of the year.' Dougan put his money where his mouth was, devoting much of Northern Arts' contingency and marketing funds, plus an accumulated surplus, to haul the cinema out of debt, on the simplest of grounds: 'The cinema is worth saving.'

There are two ways of looking at this. One is that it seems to prove Phil Penfold's assertion that Sheila Whitaker was a canny politician:

'She had a wicked smile and rather naughty charm. She had a way with her – manipulative in the best sense. She handled the old farts on her board and at Northern Arts quite brilliantly – she got money when no one else would have done.'

The other interpretation is that Whitaker was perhaps not quite so skilled – or perhaps interested – in handling budget detail as she was at programming and managing her young team. That at least is the view of the admiring John Bradshaw, one of Penfold's so-called 'old farts'.

In any event, her qualities were recognised inside and outside the North East. In addition to everything else, Whitaker had opened Cinema 2 on a regular basis, appointed an education officer, started screening films by local companies Amber and Trade, with Maggi Hurt's help opened a bookshop and information service in the old Tyne Room, publishing monographs and books, and re-opened the Coffee Rooms. As a result, in June 1983 the cinema was awarded the BFI Special Award for 'the vitality of its contribution to film education and exhibition'. Sheila accepted the award from Richard Attenborough. The following year she was headhunted by the National Film Theatre to programme its cinemas and returned to London, where she also later ran the London Film Festival for nine years. For the last decade or more Sheila has programmed film festivals all around the world, but retains a very soft spot for Newcastle.

Above: The cinema bookshop once occupied the Tyne Room – now morphed into the Digital Lounge.

'I had a lovely time there,' she says. 'I loved the area around the cinema, Grey Street and the Monument. It always had the feel of an Italian city to me – elegant and grand.'

The work of these two very different women, Hibbin and Whitaker, as successive directors had relaunched and stabilised the Tyneside Cinema, but what was the place like for its growing audience? How did the Tyneside match up as a cultural destination and visitor attraction?

Jonathan Blackie came to Newcastle to work for the city council in 1981. He arrived from Edinburgh, a place with all the cultural attractions of a capital city, albeit a small one.

'To be honest, back then Newcastle had a lot less going for it. There was Northern Stage and Live Theatre but often they were dark and had nothing on, but there was always something on at the Tyneside, even or especially on a dark night in November. It was one of the few places you could go to that wasn't a pub. So it was a refuge, a real redeeming feature.'

Not that it was exactly a luxurious refuge...

'It was damp, dingy and stank a bit, especially the loos. The seats were very uncomfortable, and the sound quality wasn't great with the Metros rattling underneath. But despite all that or maybe because of it, the place had a kind of raffish atmosphere, with people smoking Embassy Regals and roll-ups in the dark.'

The staff – especially the front-of-house staff – added to that atmosphere. The cinema wasn't perhaps what's now called a customer-focused organisation. Jonathan Blackie recalls that it seemed to be run for the benefit of the staff, in the sense that 'we were more concerned about their welfare than they were about ours'.

In particular he remembers an elderly usherette called Ivy Setterberg, who was usually dressed in a trouser suit and one of a myriad of head-scarves.

'Ivy was in her sixties and a lovely and very singular person. She prowled around Cinema 2, took your ticket in quite a challenging way, and made sure you left promptly at the end of the film. But sometimes the lights would go up and she'd be dozing in a seat, and we'd tiptoe out. She was there for years.'

Chronicle critic Phil Penfold remembers other members of staff:

'There was a projectionist called Harry Allen, who was heroic at keeping knackered old projectors going, a lovely, elegant woman called Olive Turner in the box office with a broad Geordie accent. The cleaners used to barge into critics' viewings and make derisive comments about the film before clashing out with their mops and buckets. The place was full of delightful, eccentric people.'

Above: Usherette Ivy Setterberg, sporting one of her many head-scarves.

And then there were the films.

'I must have seen hundreds there over the years. Sheila Whitaker seemed to me a bit metropolitan in her attitudes – there was a slight feeling of this is what we think you should watch – but she did put on lots of good things. I remember a screening of Bertolucci's *1900* – all six hours of it. What can I say? It was a window on the world from a cinema seat. The Tyneside made Newcastle distinctive and enriched my life. I treasured it and still do,' says Jonathan Blackie, who now heads Government Office North East.

In a way it's easy to quantify the effect of the Tyneside's principal purpose – the showing of films: the number of bums on seats. Less easy to pin down are the results of some of the other initiatives made by Hibbin and Whitaker, especially in film education. So it's interesting then to reflect on the story of another Tyneside customer in the Eighties – Patrick Collerton, then a schoolboy:

'I was at St Cuthbert's, and the Tyneside was where we'd meet girls from the Sacred Heart for a first date. I liked it – it was homely and mildly bohemian, but I didn't go that much, unlike my mum and dad. Like everyone else I had my *Betty Blue* poster on the wall and went to *Rocky Horror Show* screenings, when everyone jumped on stage, but I was more into entertainment as a kid – *Star Wars* and the like. The Tyneside was just too rarified for me.'

Then – some time in 1984, aged 14 – Patrick went on a weekend course at the cinema, an introduction to film for young people.

'At school the best you could achieve was a British Gas scholarship to Oxford, but this little course established the idea of a career in film and TV not as a pie in the sky thing but as something possible. A young producer came up from London, a bit of a wide-boy he was, but he talked about stories with such passion and brio. A woman from Tyne Tees showed us how to do make-up – scars and things. We watched films and talked about them. This was so important to me, the idea of a career in this business wasn't so daunting – no longer a dark art, this could be something for me.'

After university, Patrick returned to Newcastle and set up his own production company. He won an International Emmy for his Channel 4 documentary *The Boy Whose Skin Fell Off*, has made prize-winning ad campaigns and just directed his first network TV drama, *Joe Maddison's War* for ITV.

In appointing Sheila Whitaker's successor as director, the Tyneside's trustees broke a pattern that their predecessors had established in securing Nina Hibbin and then her: they didn't appoint someone with film programming experience.

Fred Brookes had originally studied fine art at Newcastle University in the Sixties and stayed on to teach there. He'd visited the Film Theatre in its early days – indeed he'd briefly gone out with Rachel Scott, one of Dixon Scott Junior's daughters – before returning to his native East Midlands to help set up an arts centre.

When he returned to Newcastle as director of the cinema in 1985 and made his first tour of the building, he had one over-riding impression:

Above: Charlton Heston flanked by two successive cinema directors, Fred Brookes right, and Peter Packer left.

'It was a very brown cinema – everything had been painted dark chocolate. It was very shabby. The other major concern was the financial position – Tyne Wear County Council had always been a great supporter but that had been abolished by Mrs Thatcher and the City Council was under pressure and wanted to cut our grant, so we had to fight a campaign against that, which was partly successful.'

In his relatively short time as director – just over two years – Brookes also grasped a nettle that had become increasingly painful to the cinema. He abolished the life membership programme, and the great advantages that came with it.

'It was an amazing deal for people, but made no sense for us. Our finances were on a knife-edge, but our best supporters were really taking from us, not contributing to us. It had to go.'

Even more controversial was an accompanying measure that affected people like Mike Mould – actor, performer, founder of the theatre company Bruvvers and in large part creator of what's now the Ouseburn cultural quarter.

His former partner Ali Rhind explains:

'For quite a few years Mike used to drum up custom for the children's screenings on Saturdays. He'd stand outside the cinema dressed as PC Plod, in a big hat and brandishing an even bigger truncheon, then start the children's films with jokes and silliness of one sort or another. He got paid in free tickets and then a life membership. This unfortunately disappeared in the Eighties when the management changed.'

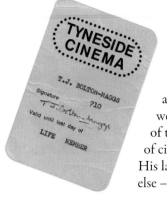

Some questioned how a something called a life membership could summarily be withdrawn, but Brookes pressed on with his changes, aided by a new management tool – an early Apple Macintosh computer, which had only just appeared on the market. He regularly sold ice-creams in Cinema 1 – to help get to know his audience better – and began to feel that those much-vaunted festivals were maybe not such a good thing after all: 'They sucked money out of the cinema and were perhaps run for the benefit of a small coterie of cinéastes.' But Brookes' initial momentum as director began to stall. His lack of experience in programming meant he had to hire someone else – Peter Packer – to do the job instead. There were other issues:

Above: Lifetime membership card terminated early.

'I had a bad run-in with David Isaacs, arts editor of the *Journal*, who took a very negative and personal view of what I was doing. It was a difficult final year. I was going through a divorce, trying to sell our house, my mother died, I was struggling with the cinema's finances and in the end kind of made myself redundant. So I left Newcastle and returned to my roots in Nottingham.'

Peter Packer, the man who replaced Fred Brookes as director, remembers the switch slightly differently. He says the trustees, through its chairman Roger Neville, offered him the top job while Fred was on holiday, on condition that he broke the news to his former boss on his return. Packer wasted no time, redecorating the director's office and installing himself in it, with his own fixtures and fittings, paintings and books. The room later became known to staff as the 'headmaster's study'. A new management style swept through the cinema, in keeping with the temper of the times and the nature of the coming man. Out, for instance, went Fred's ponytail and preference for the casual look, and in came a power dresser, with pinstripe suit and tie, and with a typical detail, 'a pair of well-polished Church's shoes'. This was after all the 1980s...

Peter Packer had studied for his PhD at Durham and stayed in the North East, firstly to teach in adult education at Newcastle University, and then lecture in film at the polytechnic.

He lived in Spital Tongues, a near-neighbour of T Dan Smith, who'd recently been released from prison after his corruption conviction: they had some interesting conversations over the garden fence. He'd first been taken on at the Tyneside by Sheila Whitaker as a part-time education officer, before being given the programming job by Fred Brookes. When he became director, he swiftly renamed the job title 'director-programmer', which was a clue to his approach. Packer believed the urgent priority wasn't cultural, but financial and managerial:

Above: Peter Packer's publicity shot.

'I remember I went to see our accountant, a rather gloomy old-timer, and he told me later that when I appeared from the lift in a suit, he began to think the cinema might actually have a future. I knew it had to be run as a business. Early on I opened a letter in error (I swear!) for the Coffee Rooms. It was a hefty tax bill, which meant they were doing well, so I doubled the rent. There were 36 full-time and part-time staff – a third of them had to be made redundant, which was hard. The wife of one projectionist who left one year from retirement told me she hated me, because he was always under her feet now. Later he confessed he appreciated the extra time he had with his grandchildren. I went in early one morning to find a gaggle of Scotswood Road cleaners in pinnies and head-scarves, not working in the cinema but holed up smoking and drinking mugs of tea in a café round the corner. Their rather fierce leader said, it's a fair cop, Peter. No one had ever questioned why we needed five cleaners, but I did. It was like that Fifties film *I'm All Right, Jack*, the difference being I was no Ian Carmichael.'

Wielding his managerial new broom, Packer was helped by two factors: by the late Eighties, the economy was growing and money flowing more easily; and the increasing popularity, and move into the mainstream, of films like *Diva*, *Betty Blue* and a stream of limpidly beautiful Merchant-Ivory pieces that proved attractive to young audiences. The Tyneside was becoming sexy and cool.

The festival began to change too, as Packer remembers:

'There'd been a tendency to put on films about life in tower-blocks in Warsaw, but no one went to see them. I put on a season of films based on operas and the cinema was pretty much the first in the UK to show films by Almodóvar and other Spanish directors. We had a Spanish-themed festival, in which we introduced gay films to Newcastle.

Above: Cinema staff and a swirling carpet, photographed for 'Screen', 6 March 1990.

There was press hysteria – the *Daily Star* was camped outside my house, the city council got its knickers in a twist, and my board went missing – they were very nervous. *Tras el Cristal* by Agustí Villaronga, a disturbing film about a Nazi paedophile, had no certificate and would have had to go to the Newcastle Licensing Committee if they'd called it in. In fact they didn't, but instead called in a totally innocent film about a man getting onto the New York subway dressed as a penis, just to see how people reacted. They passed that and the row calmed down, partly because I submitted a resumé of the paedophile film that was somewhat economical with the truth. I could have got into big trouble if someone had complained, but they didn't. I got away with it.'

If all this sounds rather stressful, it was. Packer obviously had great fun running the Tyneside. He lists some highlights: 'serving on the festival jury with Julie Christie, very sweet and earnest; getting the Duke of Northumberland as patron, a bit of a nutter but mad about film; Derek Jarman, an always enthusiastic mentor.' The cinema had been redecorated, a disabled ramp installed, the loos no longer stank. Of more dubious value, the entrance arcade had been glazed in, its mosaic and terrazzo floors tiled over, and the main entrance moved to High Friar Lane. The project over-ran in time and money and many people loathed the new look, but Packer pressed on, fortified by new and larger audiences and the fact that the Tyneside was actually making a profit. But he paid the price with his health. The day before he returned home from a holiday in the US, the comparatively young Peter Packer had a heart attack. He decided to change his life, and in 1991 made a premature departure, leaving the programming of the cinema to a young protégé, Briony Hanson.

'Peter had taught me on my film course at Newcastle Poly and we both ended up later at the Tyneside. I suppose he was my mentor and so he was rarely mean to me but sometimes wicked to others. I thought he was funny and brilliant, but his people skills could be a little lacking. I guess he was a man in a hurry – he just wanted to take the Tyneside out of its rather sleepy library status.'

Trustee Chris Hurt was sorry to see him go too: 'He was a barrel of fun at meetings, sharp and clever – a very attractive character in a very demanding job.'

But let's leave the last word to projectionist Ray Reed, who's becoming a kind of Greek chorus in this history of the Tyneside Cinema. He offers his own judgement of the crowded and controversial Packer years:

'Everybody liked Packer, though he was a bit irritating because you could never win an argument with him. He was an ex-public schoolboy who could charm the birds out of the trees. He was very social, a great character, and a great bullshitter. He was all right, Peter.'

Previous directors of the cinema had either retired or gone on to other jobs in the culture business. Peter Packer did things differently.

After a heart bypass, he became a Benedictine monk for the next ten years, later taking an MBA and setting up a thriving media consultancy. The cycle has turned again and he's just become parish priest at St John Chrysostom, in south London.

From Peckham, Peter Packer casts a blessing on the Tyneside.

'It wasn't easy making people redundant. We were under constant threat of bankruptcy. It was an incredibly steep learning curve and I felt I was always under pressure. I could be flippant and say it almost broke my heart, but really I loved the old place.'

I spent the 1980s away from Tyneside, living and working in London, returning occasionally for family celebrations, holidays by the sea, football matches, the odd play of mine opening at Live Theatre, the funeral of my dad, who was a Tyneside regular...

During these trips I usually caught a film at the cinema with him and other members of the family, maybe two or three times a year: an occasional pleasure rather than a habit. So to catch a flavour of those years, I asked two writers who grew up on Tyneside in that decade to write about the cinema that came to mean a great deal to both, in myriad ways.

My thanks to Elaine Cusack and Lee Hall: they've written very different pieces, but with many common strands, not least the importance of a good cheese savoury...

Elaine Cusack

'I never know when I'm going to need a Horlicks...'

Above: Elaine Cusack and her soulmate, Kim, standing on the hill opposite Live Theatre (now Newcastle Crown Court) in 1985.

Courtesy of Elaine Cusack

It was Kim Warren, my effortlessly cool friend, who introduced me to the Tyneside in the mid 1980s. Kim will hate me for describing her as cool but it's true. I was 14 and she was in the year below me at school when we began to acknowledge each other. It wasn't The Done Thing to hang around with younger kids but ours was a friendship waiting to happen.

Kim and I had matching short spiky hair and shared a love of music. I think we first started chatting at an Everything But The Girl gig. Soon we were swapping handwritten notes and spending our lunchtimes planning weekend explorations of Newcastle's cultural and architectural hotspots.

Kim was a member of the Tyneside (see, I told you she was cool) and the first film we watched together was a Friday night screening of *Paris, Texas*. Kim is vegetarian and I decided to give up meat after that first Tyneside experience. My decision had nothing to do with Harry Dean Stanton's acting or the Ry Cooder soundtrack and everything to do with this new kind of friendship. Kim and I were shedding our adolescent skin and exploring beliefs and ideas that would help shape our adult lives. The Tyneside was our primary source of cultural nourishment. One of the highlights of that period was the Tyneside's 1985 film festival.

Kim and I bought tickets for the opening night's screening of *My Beautiful Laundrette*. When we arrived we spotted the film's lead, Daniel Day-Lewis, in the foyer. We giggled and nudged our way to our seats but there was more excitement in store. Daniel, Our Beautiful Actor, came and sat in front of us! It was both thrilling and disconcerting to watch him on the big screen that night.

A gay relationship lies at the heart of *Laundrette* and it didn't take long for me to realise the importance of the Tyneside to the local gay community. It was the first public place I observed same-sex couples holding hands. The shelf on the left hand side of the entrance hall played a vital role in the lives of local gay men and women. It was regularly stocked with copies of the *Pink Paper* and flyers advertising lesbian and gay events.

I loved that entrance hall shelf. I used to perch myself on it and read the Tyneside's brochure. In summer 1986 I left flyers advertising my first poetry pamphlet on the shelf. The flyers were black and white photocopies of a handwritten press release, accompanied by a photograph of the author aged two.

The Tyneside offered me so much: late night shows, double bills and a blind eye to smuggled booze! I liked to browse in the shop on the first floor. It stocked fantastic greetings cards, posters and T-shirts. In 1988 I was asked to perform my poetry at London's South Bank Centre. I was very nervous and ended up wearing my treasured *Betty Blue* T-shirt. My Tyneside Cinema comfort blanket helped me through the poetry reading.

I was always intrigued by the Tyne Room. One evening in 1987 I was leaving the cinema when a man approached me and asked if I'd heard of Britain's oldest socialist party. I said I hadn't and he invited me to a meeting of the Socialist Party of Great Britain in the Tyne Room. The meeting was sparsely attended but I was fired up. 'When does the revolution start?' I quipped, as other attendees politely shuffled their feet.

I can't write about my favourite cinema without mentioning the Tyneside Coffee Rooms. I fell for this café the first time I walked through the doors over 25 years ago. I was impressed by the mix of clientele: old ladies in hats, students, gay couples and lone diners reading books. This café was very different from, say, Mark Toney's or department store self-service restaurants. The Coffee Rooms attracted diners who were prepared to share tables. I loved the fact I never knew who or what to expect as I walked up the stairs to the Coffee Rooms. It was and still is a terrific place to people-watch.

↗
3rd FLOOR
Cinema 2/Club
2nd FLOOR
TYNESIDE
COFFEE ROOMS
Tyne Room
1st FLOOR
Bookshop &
Information Centre
Video Viewing/
Education

Above: Elaine Cusack's retrieved sign. In the top right corner are the remains of a sticker advertising Rock Against Racism or Anti-Apartheid Movement.

My favourite order in the 1980s was a pot of Earl Grey tea for one and a red Penguin biscuit. It had to be a red rather than a blue wrapped biscuit. Don't ask me why. One Saturday lunchtime I ordered a cheese savoury roll. I didn't touch my side salad and the thin student beside me asked: 'Please can I have your side salad?' I nodded, then pushed my plate towards him but this experience almost put me off further education. Would I have to beg for salad if I passed my A levels and secured a place at university?

The Tyneside Coffee Rooms remain my venue of choice for brunch, lunch or afternoon cuppa. Although Horlicks is no longer on the menu, my friendly waiter Jeffrey assures me I can still order it. I find that comforting. I never know when I'm going to need a Horlicks.

I'm proud to say I own a piece of Tyneside Cinema history. I was leaving the Tyneside one Saturday afternoon in the summer of 1985 or 1986 when I spotted a skip in High Friar Lane. It was piled high with office furniture from the Tyneside. Sticking out of the top was the painted wooden information sign that used to hang at the bottom of the stairs on the ground floor. I looked around for policemen or snitches lurking in doorways then yanked it out. I'm certain I saw a Bakelite phone and some ledgers in the skip but I knew I couldn't carry anything else. I had a long walk home from Felling Metro ahead of me. Uphill all the way.

Below: Lee Hall

Courtesy of Lee Hall

University took me away from my favourite cinema in 1989 and a variety of jobs kept me tied to London for the following two decades. I returned to the North East in 2009 and reacquainted myself with the Tyneside. Nowadays I live a Metro ride away from Pilgrim Street and the wooden sign I fished out of the skip is firmly screwed to my hallway wall. Oh yes, and dear Kim remains my treasured friend.

Lee Hall

'It was uncharted, mysterious but had a vital allure...'

The Tyneside Cinema first came into my consciousness because of the fame of its Coffee Rooms. If you were 14 in Newcastle in the early Eighties, the Tyneside Coffee Rooms were the height of sophistication. I suppose before we could easily frequent the Strawberry or the Trent House it was the Coffee Rooms where one could meet like-minded souls, or at least wear your long scarves in their company. There were aesthetes from Jesmond, the People's Theatre – people from all over. Anyway, it didn't seem to matter that this sophistication manifested itself in a Cheese Savoury – it was a place of metropolitan romance.

I started going regularly to the Tyneside when I was about 15. An older friend of mine, Mikey Kelly, who's now an art lecturer, used to come round on a Sunday night and insist I got the bus into town with him. Whether simply no one else would go with him to see the esoteric fare at hand, or whether he just understood that seeing these things would change my life I don't know. But he made it his business to make sure I went.

I think the first thing I saw was *The Tin Drum,* which I found dazzling. It was pretty cool to be watching 'European' movies – these must be good because they had subtitles. But they were good. Every Sunday we saw more, sometimes they were double bills, I think. I remember it was mostly 'art-house' fare but I had no idea of the term or the concept back then – they were just vividly imaginative films. Eric Rohmer, Fassbinder, all the greats were there.

I also remember going to see a five-hour documentary about a Buddhist temple which culminated in a monk being burned in the lotus position and the resultant pyre was filmed until the flames went out. I can't remember whether he was dead or alive. I think that he was alive at the outset but I wonder whether I've conflated it with the famous images from the Vietnam War. Anyway, I remember sitting through this gruesome zen epic mesmerised.

There weren't that many people who went to such showings – but to those that were there I think they were probably disproportionately influential. Nearly all the actors, writers, directors and artists who have subsequently emerged from Tyneside seemed to be avid patrons.

These were the days before you could get this stuff on video – so seeing it 'somewhere' was crucial. It was also, of course, later a place to catch the more interesting movies on general release but it was this programming of one-offs that I loved most. I also loved the typed sheets they used to give you. If you were 15 and from Walkerville you didn't really know how to find out about the films you were watching. I couldn't afford the books in the bookshop – it was a whole other world teeming with names I didn't know – so getting it piecemeal was quite useful.

I also remember being taken to see some Lindsay Kemp films when I was in the sixth form. I suppose I thought it was normal to have such easy

Above: David Bennent in Volker Schlöndorff's 'The Tin Drum'.

access to Buddhist documentaries or avant-garde gay dance troupes. Little did I know what a unique micro-climate I was growing up in. It's pretty much impossible to find this stuff now, even on YouTube.

And the posters also held some strange aura. I had some on my bedroom wall. I can't even remember where the images were from. There was something decadent about the place though – whether I associated the Thirties architecture with some Weimar decadence I don't know. I've a feeling Louise Brooks was on one of the posters, and maybe Abel Gance's *Napoleon*. But the main thing was that it promised another world beyond the clod-footed realities of Tyneside – a world of imagination and sensuality. Depictions of lives which were sophisticated because their emotional range was not simply just about getting by, or conforming, what was celebrated on the posters and in the films were the possibilities of life, of other ways of living. Even though they were distant and no doubt fantasies – you could sort of have a bit of them by buying a poster, or letting them glance your humdrum life of a Sunday evening.

I was not a film buff, I was more of a dilettante – and the Tyneside importantly fitted in with a nexus of cultural places and experiences: the Trent House jukebox, the youth theatres, the Side Gallery and Cinema, the Bookhouse bookshop and its downstairs cafe. These were all the places one could rub up against culture in one's secondhand Oxfam overcoat.

The more I go on and spend time living in the great metropolises of the world (I am writing this from NYC), I realise how privileged my cultural life was growing up on Tyneside – how easy it was to find the avant-garde, the classics, how most of my aesthetic education was formed way before I got to university. And of course how joyous it was to find all this – almost by accident – for the first time. It was uncharted, mysterious but had a vital allure. Thank god I didn't really know what I was supposed to think or who these people were. I just watched cos it was there, it was easy to get to, and it was fabulous fun.

Opposite page: Tyneside Cinema masquerading as Metro station, 1990s.

8 | 'A cross between a country solicitor's and Grace Brothers...'

For the Tyneside Cinema the 1990s and 2000s were a game of two halves. The last ten years of the 20th century for the cinema were years of managerial drift, in which the years when there actually was a director in charge were outnumbered by those without, the fabric of the building was increasingly unfit for purpose, and the figures on the balance sheet were increasingly in red. Fundamentally, the place wasn't working.

The decade following the millennium saw a phoenix-like rising up: a period of stabilisation, then the huge gamble of redevelopment, temporary removal to the other side of the Tyne Bridge and finally, not so much a re-birth as a reinvention totally in the style and spirit of the cinema's founding father, Dixon Scott.

This was only possible for two main reasons: as had always been the case in its history, when the chips were down the cinema somehow found the right people at the right time to do what was needed, and was also able to call on the undying, quietly passionate support of its audience. Then again, 'support' seems a bit limp. What the hell – this is the movies and we're into the final reel. Let's just call it love.

As the 1990s began, the Tyneside was in good shape. The building had been renovated with a new entrance in High Friar Lane (albeit not to everyone's taste, especially given the further despoiling of the original Persian decor), the programming had caught the wave of the increasing popularity in the 1980s of what might be called 'soft art-house', its management was stable, competent and sometimes inspired. As a result, the cinema had made a profit, paid off its debts and even built up cash reserves. This was more or less unprecedented since the day in 1968 when the screening of *Hugs and Kisses* had started a new era in the history of the old News Theatre.

Much of the credit for this happy state of affairs goes to the cinema's director for the previous five years, Peter Packer. An inspiration to some, bully to others, Packer managed every facet of the cinema with determination and fierce attention to detail. Only one previous director – Nina Hibbin – had tried to carry such a burden: it wore her out within three years and she retired. Packer kept up a murderous pace for five years and then his body called a halt. He had a heart attack and left the Tyneside within weeks.

Packer's departure left a void that the cinema's trustees didn't fill properly for eight years. Their difficulty is understandable: the managerial model that had been proven to work best by previous directors, Packer especially, was a combination of programmer and manager.

The problem was that very few people had the intellect, experience and physical energy to carry it off.

Suzy Varty, an artist and cartoonist who'd been first taken to the News Theatre at her age of three by her cousins in the mid Fifties, was a trustee throughout the 1990s:

'Basically, we lurched from crisis to crisis for years. After Peter Packer left we couldn't seem to find a director who could both programme and manage the business. This wasn't easy, but it could be done. In the end we made appointments we shouldn't have made, and didn't make appointments we should have made. The result was a kind of lost decade for the cinema.'

In the immediate aftermath of Packer's departure, these roles were temporarily filled by Briony Hanson. Hanson had first come to work at the cinema as a student in the early Eighties – riding shotgun on Saturday morning kids' shows – and found her true vocation.

'When I went to college, I had no idea what I wanted to be. But when I discovered the Tyneside, I fell in love with it, and the idea of working in film. When I left the poly, Peter took me on and over the years I think I must have done every job in the cinema, from usherette to director, with the exception of projection. I was an usherette, I cleaned, ran the box office and the bookshop. But I loved programming best.'

But Hanson didn't get the director's job on a permanent basis, at least not yet. In 1993 the board hired Roy Bristow, a Londoner who'd previously managed a small independent cinema in Rupert Street, the Metro, but the appointment didn't work out for either side and he left after a year. Then the trustees did give the job to Briony Hanson, but that too was short-lived. She quickly left to take a job at the BFI, running their Information Unit, and is now director of the Script Factory, the film development agency.

Above: Briony Hanson, Tyneside Cinema's programmer and then director following the resignation of Peter Packer.

'I loved being director the first time. It was bliss doing the programming and I felt the staff was behind me. The only thing I didn't enjoy was doing the rota for the projectionists!

'But then Roy Bristow came and went and when I got the job properly, it didn't feel quite the same. It felt like I'd already done it. I'd been there maybe too long – I'd only ever worked at the Tyneside – and then my partner got a job in London and I was headhunted by the BFI, and it just felt right to go.'

In the mid Nineties, Jonny Tull was beginning a career at the Tyneside that would take him from usher to programme manager, the job that Briony Hanson was doing when he arrived.

'Briony was great, highly focused, really on the ball with her programming. Those early years are still with me. We had a lot of success with new film-makers, people like Tarantino. Whenever I watch *Pulp Fiction* today – and I watched it again recently – I feel the moment near the end when I had to open the doors for the audience to leave. I suppose I'm hard-wired to be an usher forever.'

But increasingly these programming successes were being undermined by financial worries, as well as the declining fabric of the building, symbolised for gallery director Mara-Helen Wood by the rat she saw scurrying down the centre aisle one night in the mid Nineties, appropriately enough during the screening of Brian de Palma's horror film, *The Fury*.

After Briony Hanson left, it again took the trustees a long time to find a replacement, but eventually they appointed Kath Baker, who had considerable experience in cinema programming, most recently in Leeds. Her tenure ended sooner than anyone expected. The decisive moment arrived in 1998 when the trustees were summoned to a meeting at Northern Arts headquarters in Archbold Terrace in Jesmond. Among them was Geoff Cook, solicitor by training and recently retired chief executive of Newcastle City Council:

Above: Kath Baker, Tyneside Cinema's director, late 1990s.

Opposite page from top to bottom: Tyneside Cinema trustees proclaiming their favourite movies, from top: Suzy Varty, Sue Wilkinson, Simon Elliott, Geoff Cook and Graham Randall.

Photos © Keith Pattison

'I became concerned about the lack of reliable financial information. I was aware there was a significant though not massive debt, but by the next board it had appeared to double, and I began to suspect we were actually trading illegally and the management didn't have a grip on the money.'

Another trustee, Simon Elliott, confirms this analysis: 'Kath was a creative person, not a manager. It's hard to describe the culture of the organisation at that time, but I'd say it was somewhat hand-knitted.'

Suzy Varty was at the fateful meeting in Jesmond:

'That year I had a heart attack and missed a meeting. At the next one Kath Baker told everyone we were in serious debt and we had to sack some members of staff. Everyone was very concerned but we never quite got to the bottom of how it had happened.'

What happened next changed the history of the Tyneside Cinema: a small group of trustees – Suzy Varty calls them a 'cabal' – went to the pub for a stiff drink.

'There were four of us – Geoff Cook, Graham Randall, who had a lifetime of experience of business with Greggs, Simon Elliott, who worked at Procter & Gamble, and me. We looked at each other and said, what are we going to do?' says Suzy.

'We had a choice – resign or stay and fight. Personally I didn't want to be part of a failing organisation which was being run unprofessionally. In the end, we decided to give it a go,' says Geoff Cook, who had the time and now the inclination to try to turn things around. When BBC producer Sue Wilkinson stepped down as chair, he took over. Initially the job was tricky and messy. Director Kath Baker and two other senior members of staff left soon afterwards.

Sadly Kath Baker is no longer here to give her side of this story, but I'm happy to report one way in which she left a permanent and positive mark on the cinema: it was she who persuaded two distinguished film directors to become patrons of the Tyneside – local boy Mike Figgis, and Mike Hodges, whose rushes for *Get Carter* were once screened for him and his star Michael Caine in the old Cinema 2.

Yet again, there was some delay before Baker's replacement arrived, but this time the trustees got the appointment unquestionably right. Mark Dobson entered the Tyneside story.

Dobson spent his early childhood in Gateshead. His dad was a chippy, mostly working in the South East. One day his cousin Susan took him to the Odeon opposite the Tyneside to see *Chitty Chitty Bang Bang* and while his mother was doing the ironing afterwards, she asked him how he'd feel about moving south. As a result, Mark grew up in Battersea and Milton Keynes, but returned north in the early Eighties to start a degree in fine art at Newcastle University – and experienced the familiar epiphany of Geordies returning home.

'Crossing the High Level on the train that first time, looking at the bridges and the city, I got that tingly feeling – I immediately felt at home,' he says. 'I discovered the Tyneside via a stall at freshers' week and came down to buy a poster for my room, like thousands of others. I came obsessively in the Eighties – it was the scene of many failed dates. *Betty Blue*, of course, and Coppola's *One From the Heart*, which the critics hated but I loved. I remember floating out afterwards.'

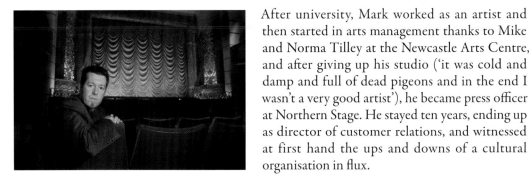

After university, Mark worked as an artist and then started in arts management thanks to Mike and Norma Tilley at the Newcastle Arts Centre, and after giving up his studio ('it was cold and damp and full of dead pigeons and in the end I wasn't a very good artist'), he became press officer at Northern Stage. He stayed ten years, ending up as director of customer relations, and witnessed at first hand the ups and downs of a cultural organisation in flux.

Above: Mark Dobson, Tyneside Cinema's chief executive, from 2000.

'It was a hugely enjoyable and very challenging experience. After ten years I began to feel that I'd progressed as far as I could. I began to wonder if I had it in me to run an arts organisation.'

Mark Dobson began to answer his own question when he started work as the Tyneside Cinema's new chief executive in January 2000. He had stopped being a Tyneside regular in the 1990s – 'the programme wasn't quite as interesting and the building off-putting' – but one Sunday afternoon, the day before his interview, he turned up to watch David Lynch's *The Straight Story*.

'I knew the Tyneside was in trouble – everyone in Newcastle's arts scene did – and I knew enough to know that if I got the job, turning the cinema around would have to take over my life for a time. That Sunday the cinema was near empty, but I fell in love with the Tyneside again and went in to the interview convinced that the place was worth the effort that it would undoubtedly require. Looking back I probably underestimated just how hard a task it was going to be.'

Dobson had made his own diagnosis of the job facing him and came up with a lengthy list of pressing issues. But the starting point was that he and his contemporaries had lost the Tyneside habit.

'We were perhaps representative of the audience it had lost. After years of drift, the pictures hadn't got small, but somehow the Tyneside had.

'With no senior management in place, audiences waning and the constant threat of funding cuts on the horizon, it was unsurprisingly very inward-looking, almost scared of its own shadow. The staff had taken pay cuts to keep the business running and was disenchanted. Relations with funders were poor and there was little sense of leadership. The festival had been quietly allowed to die. It wasn't generating new audiences. The building was romantic but tatty. We weren't paying the bills, and when I arrived and for the next two years or so, it was often a week-by-week struggle to find money to pay the wages. We had to run just to stand still.'

The trustees' determination to tackle these problems at the cinema and the recruitment of a new chief executive – the new title was significant – bought a period of grace with the funders, especially the BFI who, for a while at least, removed the threat of grant cuts.

Some of the issues would need time, but Dobson and his team embarked on some swift firefighting. The programming was tweaked to ensure that successful films (*Being John Malkovich,* for instance) were brought back for second, third and even fourth runs. With the help of the BFI the cinema also acquired *American Beauty* on its UK release, which made both a splash and a lot of money. The staff was restructured and Jonny Tull was appointed publicity officer. Marketing was smartened: access to an improved mailing list was made free, which soon ensured that ten times the number of people were receiving the cinema's brochures. Hardly surprisingly, in no time at all there was a 10 per cent increase in audiences. Equally encouraging, a new Friends scheme was quickly launched and within weeks 500 people signed up (beginning a long climb to the current total close to 4,000). The Tyneside audience proved its loyalty once again.

With the help of a re-motivated staff, Dobson's 100-day survival plan worked. But how to make it thrive?

Enter the extraordinary Roy Pattison.

He and Mark Dobson had previously worked together at Northern Stage in the Nineties, when Dobson had hired Roy as a marketing consultant.

'Across an intensive year of work together – there was no other work than intensive with Roy – he became my friend and my mentor. I pretty much tore up everything I'd learned about marketing in the arts at that point and started again.'

Pattison's theatre roots went back to the 1960s when he worked as a stage manager at Joan Littlewood's Stratford East company. In the Eighties he worked in commercial marketing and then helped set up London's alternative listings magazine *City Limits* and establish the house style that went with it. He later worked for a number of experimental artists in the US and UK but had become disenchanted with arts politics. Despite this, in the summer of 2000 he pitched up in Newcastle with a mission to help Dobson reposition the Tyneside Cinema for the 21st century.

'One day, soon after my arrival at the Tyneside, we got back in touch via the still relatively new medium of electronic mail – a boon for both of us as I liked writing and he *really* liked writing. A few days later, feeling very alone in the chief exec role at the cinema, I sent him an email asking if I could coax him out of retirement to come and help me. I remember I wrote that everyone here has a story about the Tyneside, the problem is that they're all old stories of past glories and I needed him to help me write some new stories. As I pressed 'Send', an email simultaneously appeared in my inbox from Roy saying he had been thinking about how I had described the Tyneside and that if I wanted some help, he might just be interested.

'So we agreed to work together again. I commissioned him initially with my own money. The cinema literally had no money at all. Months later, after presenting the board with Roy's marketing strategy, chair Geoff Cook found this out and insisted I be reimbursed.'

Most of his new colleagues were expecting a marketing consultant to appear in double-breasted suit and huge glasses, but the chain-smoking Roy wore Doc Martens and ripped denims. He soon asked Fiona Fitzpatrick, who'd first come to the cinema two years before as front-of-house manager, to work with him. They shared an office and so began a very intensive collaboration:

'He painted the floor black and the walls purple and brought in loads of Seventies furniture. He played music all the time and just poured himself into this project. He had a very imaginative way of looking at things. That doesn't really do justice to him. He was unique, a total maverick.'

The first outcome of Pattison's work was however pretty standard: the marketing consultant delivered a marketing assessment, 53 pages of it. But his readers didn't have to read very far into it to realise this was a report with a difference:

'This report is written in plain English.
It should not be read at your desk between meetings, on the bus, whilst putting the kids to bed, watching television, walking the dog, cooking a meal or during a row with a loved one.
Instead, please pour yourself a glass of wine, put on your favourite piece of music, sit in your most comfortable armchair and relax into the world of possibilities.
What has finally emerged could be best described as a history of the future. It is a strategy painted on a large canvas. It is bold and in parts, it is audacious.
It is also very achievable.
For those who spend a great deal of their professional lives reading documents such as this, much effort has been made to keep you awake.
However, should this effort prove to have been fruitless, the addendum on page 53 has been included to assist you to while away your time constructively.'

The report then gets down to business – with an elegant and witty exposition of the work of the 19th century Danish philosopher Søren Kierkegaard, with particular regard to his musings on the concept of choice. It moves on to a discussion of Marxist theory and then the art of Marcel Duchamps before returning to Kierkegaard ('There is really nothing like a Dane!') and the essence of his marketing strategy: the cinema owed a duty to the public of Tyneside to help them avoid the existential dread of choice by giving them no choice – 'the Tyneside will be their natural home for a range of cultural activities, a place in which no further choices need ever be made.'

He made it sound so simple.

Below: Roy Pattison decorated his office at Tyneside Cinema with kitsch Seventies furniture.

Pattison provided a withering list of the feelings of the staff about their work-place: 'bureaucratic', 'slow', 'unresponsive', 'smelly', 'a cross between a country solicitor's and Grace Brothers'. He came to the conclusion that the place needed more than just a shake-up, but a kind of creative reawakening, and so listed a range of recommendations, all of which were meant to provoke and excite the cinema's customers, real and potential, and its staff. It's interesting to note how many of these ideas have since become reality:

- *to use under-used or 'dead' space, and down time in the cinemas;*
- *to encourage retail activity;*
- *to promote the cinema's heritage and history, and record the reminiscences of customers;*
- *to get involved in film-making;*
- *to embrace new technology, especially the web;*
- *to use every opportunity to be creative.*

The report is full of lively language and ideas, but one striking phrase among many jumped out at me: 'As in cold-set printing, it is not the dot that produces the image it is the absence of dot. It is the absence of black that gives texture and definition. We now gradate images not in dots, but in pixels. *There are twelve million pixels in a modern cinema image.* This means that there are more than twelve million places on that image from where a pixel is absent.

Below: The origami instruction sheet which appears on the final page of Roy Pattison's marketing report for Tyneside Cinema.

The sentence in italics is a curious echo of the slogan with which Dixon Scott Senior sold his new Kino cinema in Jarrow 90 years before: 'Every picture tells a story, and there are 60,000 pictures in every Kino performance.'

Pattison made one final suggestion: the Tyneside should appoint a philosopher-in-residence ('a small but unusual method of payment should be devised'). In essence, Pattison's report was an application for this imaginary post; and he remained the cinema's resident thinker until his untimely death in 2002.

Alert readers may be wondering about the mysterious reference to Pattison's 'addendum' for the benefit of weary readers. Page 53 contains drawn instructions for an origami cat.

The first direct result of Pattison's report was typically counter-intuitive. In the run-up to Christmas 2000 the Tyneside held a party. Fiona Fitzpatrick helped organise it:

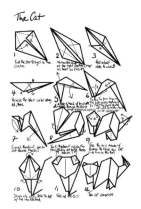

'Roy knew we had to reach out to new and younger audience – tell people the Tyneside was there, put it on the map. We came up with this idea that we should have late-night parties and invite everyone from the young arts community. We started with the Christmas party. Its flavour was slightly cheesy glam – pork pies and beer. About 400 movers and shakers came and it was great – it felt like a new beginning.'

For Mark Dobson the party was 'an astute repositioning exercise which also made me laugh! What I remember best is the look on the faces of some beleaguered members of staff who simply couldn't believe that this was happening in their building. The good news that the Tyneside Cinema was somewhere to have fun – a place for 'your passions to enjoy themselves', in Roy's phrase – seemed to spread quickly to the audiences too.'

The new chief executive was meanwhile grappling with the biggest issue of all facing the Tyneside – how to make its future sustainable? He'd inherited a report from another consultant that squarely addressed this problem and included some bullet-points of its own:

Above: The 2001 chrome and neon canopy on Pilgrim Street, by architect Tim Bailey, was a reproduction of the original design for the News Theatre.

Photo © David Williams

- *to build a third 'bring-back' cinema, to enable the Tyneside to capitalise on successful films and expand revenue;*
- *to provide customers with a decent bar, and raise the lamentably low retail spend by them;*
- *most controversial of all, to leave its city centre site and the 'albatross' of an old, unwieldy building and move to a new, purpose-built centre elsewhere on Tyneside.*

This last suggestion was profoundly troubling, especially as it was made just as – out of the blue – the Tyneside was given a Grade II listing as a building of architectural and historic interest. The underlying value of this was brought home to Mark Dobson when on holiday in Miami, he went on a tour of the art deco quarter of South Beach:

'I told the guide about the building where I worked, and the guy's jaw just dropped. There was also that fact that the Tyneside was already a destination for many people who would otherwise never set foot inside a regional film theatre – the customers of the Coffee Rooms. That was a big asset to us. We didn't want to move – our customers, our funders and our political allies didn't either – even with the extra costs of extending that site rather than starting again somewhere out of town. But it was such a big idea! Dare we do it? Eventually all of us – trustees and staff – felt we just had to try.'

Before the main feature, there were a couple of supporting shorts: two exercises in project management for Dobson and his staff, chair Geoff Cook (backed by his legal and local government experience) and the other trustees. The first was the building of the espresso bar on the ground floor, with £100,000 from the Arts Council and the Grainger Town project. Tim Bailey of xsite Architecture undid a lot of the damage caused by the 1990 refurbishment, demolishing its frontage, cladding the lower section of Newe House in stone consistent with the upper, creating the café and adding a new chrome and neon canopy on the Pilgrim Street frontage as a replica of the original. The café eventually became Intermezzo, the concession being given, despite higher bids from elsewhere, to the di Giorgi family, who cannily brought their own cakes to the interview. Then the team went to work on one of Roy Pattison's *bêtes noires*, the dead space of the Tyne Room next to the Coffee Rooms ('it sounds as if it should be next door to the Mayor's Parlour!'), and converted it with £50,000 from One North East into the Mike Figgis Digital Lounge, a valuable space for party hires (the first, rather surprisingly, for a seven-year-old girl) as well as a venue for the screening of experimental film.

Meanwhile the cinema was pushing the creative envelope in other ways. Mike Figgis, director and Tyneside patron, came to Newcastle to screen his groundbreaking film *Timecode* and painted a vivid picture of the digital revolution taking over filmmaking, distribution and exhibition. His 'just do it' message was a call to arms for the young filmmakers in the audience, as well as Dobson.

Below: Developments for the new millennium, from left: The Digital Lounge, Intermezzo Café Bar's entrance on Pilgrim Street, and The Electra after its transformation from Cinema 2.

Photos © Allan Mushen

'We wanted to open up the building, which had become so introspective, to new and younger artists. In particular we wanted to support people working with digital technology and while filmmakers were sceptical of the new technology at first, we found no shortage of artists in other media – writing, music, photography, graphic design – who'd adopted the new technology and who were eagerly waiting to get their hands on the ability to make and re-make moving image.'

Meanwhile in a bar, Roy Pattison met a young promoter called Jeff Cleverly, who, with a cohort of friends, had been taking over found spaces in the city to host art-led parties (in the Sixties they probably would have been 'happenings'). Jeff became part of the team at the Tyneside and introduced Mark and Roy to the groundbreaking VJ collective, The Light Surgeons. In 2001 Dobson won a Northern Arts grant to bring this collective of multimedia artists to the cinema to carry out a digital cinema residency, working with local artists. After its sell-out success, Jeff Cleverly suggested that the next step should be a festival to 'showcase emerging local talent alongside the best international work in digital and electronic arts' – what later became the AV Festival.

This was very much part of the Pattison-Dobson strategy to use new media in cinema down-time, and 'be creative'. Fiona Fitzpatrick worked with Roy on it:

'It introduced the idea of an interactive not passive audience. There was a mesh screen, then the Light Surgeons VJ-ing on computers, then the screen itself with these amazing images being played to a soundtrack. It was going to be a big event and Roy got into a state about the end product. He thought it was going to be terrible. He often felt like that – he was a visionary but sometimes undervalued what he was doing. In the end the event sold out and was a big success, but Roy wasn't there to see it.'

In January 2002, Roy Pattison took his own life. He was 54.

His friend and collaborator Mark Dobson pays tribute to a man who helped change the history of the Tyneside.

'I learnt so much from Roy. When he came to the Tyneside, we shared a flat and for a while, just lived and breathed how to make it work. It was all about passion for him. He made a huge difference to people and institutions, but somehow lost sight of that. He changed my life, changed me into a better person personally and professionally. In many ways I think we are still following his plan. Ten years and a whole new building later, I still dig it out occasionally to reassure myself that we are keeping the faith. His death was a terrible shock.'

Below: Innovation catalyst Jeff Cleverly (beer in hand) at a Tyneside Cinema party on 17 July 2001.

Dobson soldiered on without his friend and mentor, consumed by the task, but supported increasingly by 'several board members who recognised my relative inexperience and went out of their way to support me (they still do) and my staff. As I suspected it would, the Tyneside had taken over my life. I realised I was here for the long haul.'

Time passed – but the need to redevelop the cinema became increasingly apparent, especially after it was made clear that revenue funding for film exhibition was likely to be phased out over the years ahead. The man who delivered that unpalatable message was Tom Harvey, chief executive of the region's new screen agency, Northern Film & Media (NFM), which was set up in 2001. He helped the Tyneside take the first faltering steps towards redevelopment – and with it the possibility of bridging that funding shortfall in the future – by enrolling the cinema on a business development scheme. David Prais, the consultant who worked with Dobson, was convinced by his vision and persuaded NFM to stump up a further £25,000 to hire a much-needed project manager. He also told the trustees in no uncertain terms to 'get on with the job quickly'. Despite the positive climate of the time – and the transformation of Newcastle and Gateshead's cultural infrastructure, he was convinced the cinema needed to sharpen its elbows to succeed. It was in a sprint, not a marathon.

The cinema appointed Brian Ham as its project manager. Ham had been head of strategy at ONE North East and brought experience to the project; he was also a fan of the Tyneside. He helped create a PowerPoint presentation about why the cinema had to be redeveloped and Dobson began showing it 'to everyone and anyone we thought would listen'. Next the trustees appointed architects for the project. Fletcher Priest were based in London and Cologne, but were half-run, almost inevitably, by an ex-pat Geordie, Keith Priest. The next stage was to identify key funders.

If the Tyneside was to remain where it had been since 1968, in Dixon Scott's News Theatre, and continue as the last remaining cinema in such a building, it needed to find the excess cost of adapting the structure – with an extra floor and many renovations – as opposed to a brand new building. This amounted to around £2 million. For Mark Dobson and Geoff Cook, there was an obvious place to look.

'The Heritage Lottery Fund was critical. The business model was always going to be a struggle, especially as the cost of the project gradually rose from £3.5 million to £7.5 million. We just had to get a big chunk of money from Heritage Lottery,' says Geoff.

But getting that money was easier said than done, as Mark Dobson recalls.

'The HLF bid was a huge learning curve for everyone involved. Thanks to the advice and patience of the experts at Tyne and Wear Archives and Museums and our fundraiser Gillian Spry, we began slowly to understand not that we were merely housed in an interesting old cinema but that we are custodians of a real heritage asset and what that meant. In effect when we started the redevelopment we were the region's cultural cinema and a provider of film education projects. When we reopened in 2008 we were both of those still, but also a free heritage attraction of national significance – the last surviving newsreel cinema. This was a whole new part of our business that has profoundly changed almost every aspect of how we work.

Below: Old cinema seats make a journey to new homes the day the cinema closed for renovation, boosting the fundraising appeal.

Bottom: one of a series of photos by Helena Seget about the old cinema seats in new locations, from an exhibition called 'H11'.

'The application itself was also a huge mountain to climb. In the end four outsized lever arch files were submitted – it cost £1,500 just for the photocopying.'

In the end the Tyneside received £2.6 million from the HLF. Almost as critical was a successful bid, via Jonathan Blackie's Government Office North East, to the European Regional Development Fund. ONE North East gave solid support, and there were hefty donations from the Northern Rock Foundation and the Shears Foundation. A public appeal for donations raised nearly £38,000, a response that had an effect way beyond its size. Mark Dobson:

'The evening after we'd written to our audiences about it, a man called Sidney Stoker, a stalwart of the cinema, who'd worked here as a projectionist in the 1950s and then spent the rest of his working life as a bin man, turned up with a cheque as a donation. He handed it over at the box office saying that he wished it could be more. Very quickly we had more than 700 people giving their own money to the appeal. The total amount given wasn't huge, but the clear message about how the public valued the Tyneside was plain for local politicians to see. Every one of our subsequent fundraising ruses was met with an overwhelming response. We sold all of the old chairs from the Classic – people even bought the old carpet from the Classic and tried to buy several things we were trying to preserve!'

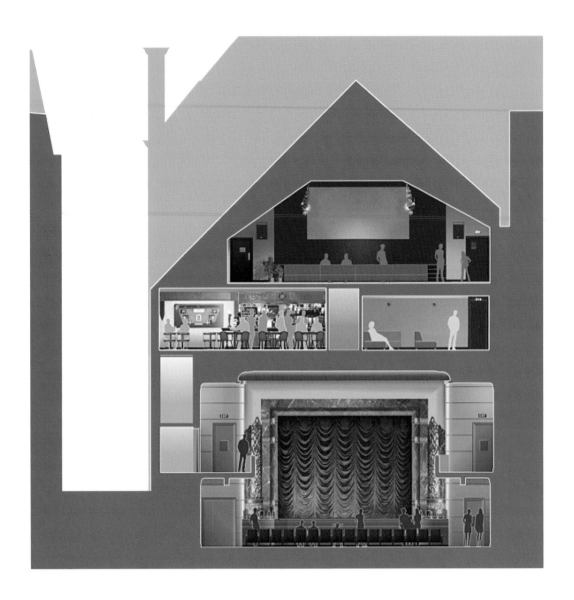

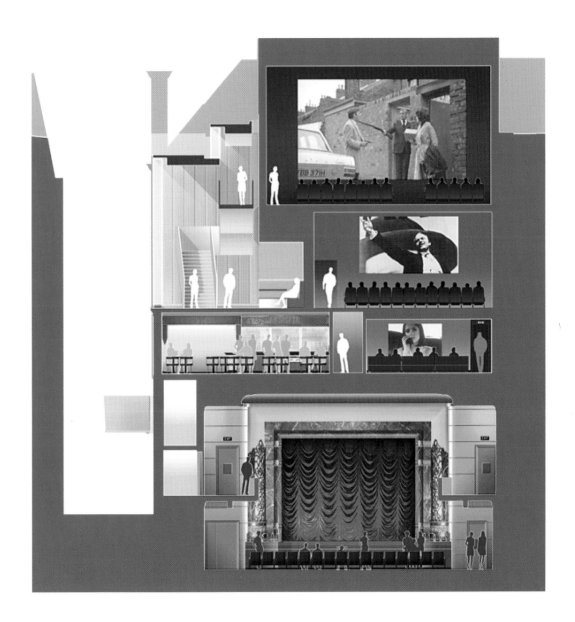

Pages 134-135: Fletcher Priest Architects' concept designs for the layout of the cinema before (left) and after (right) redevelopment.

Finally the money was ready – more or less – and on 23 November 2006 the cinema closed to let the builders in. The very last film screened was Swedish sex comedy *Hugs and Kisses*, which had so awkwardly begun the life of the Tyneside Film Theatre 40 years earlier. The very next day the Tyneside opened for business in a new home across the Tyne Bridge in Gateshead's Old Town Hall.

This wasn't originally in the script. The brutal truth of the business plan was that it made most sense – created the smallest loss – to close altogether while the building was worked on. But Dobson and his trustees began to see that this would be disaster for the cinema, for independent film exhibition in the region, and for audiences, and decided to try to find a temporary venue:

'But where? We'd no money to pay rent and to make the cinema work for the film distributors and audiences we needed a space that could work as a cinema (at little cost) and that we could have seven days a week! Lots of places were interested in having us share their theatres but what we needed was a ludicrously tall order.

Below: Tyneside Cinema's opening night party at Old Town Hall, Gateshead, on 16 November 2006.

Photo © Keith Pattison

'Then some magic happened. Anthony Sargent at The Sage Gateshead told me they'd recently vacated their temporary home in the Old Town Hall and that the council had plans to refurbish the main hall for

136

public use. He thought we might provide a great springboard for some public activity in the building if the timing worked out. A few phone calls later, thanks to the passion of the leader and chief executive of Gateshead Council, a deal was done. Despite Gateshead's generosity and the continued support of NFM and Newcastle Council, the venture still lost money – around an additional £10,000 a month over and above what we'd originally anticipated. But looking back this feels like one of the best investments the cinema has ever made.'

Others were nervous about the Gateshead move, including John Oswell, who'd also moved the Coffee Rooms, and cinema programme manager Jonny Tull:

'I was worried about the move – especially when the first week's box office was so slow, but then in the second week we played *Pan's Labyrinth* exclusively and the audience response was huge. We realised it was the programme not the venue which determined the business – and that we could make it work, and survive the closure.'

Long-standing Tyneside customers who were anxious about the Gateshead move were instantly reassured as the lights went down: on the screen they saw the familiar image of the old red curtain opening – the kind of detail, suggests trustee Simon Elliott, typical of Mark Dobson's creative leadership.

Below: Tyneside on The Toon screening of 'Life of Brian' at St Thomas's, Newcastle. One of a series of hugely popular screenings in unusual settings around the city.

On the other side of the river, a new character played his part in the Tyneside story – relatively briefly, but absolutely crucially. Jimmy Floyd (great nephew of one of the Ashington group of pitmen-painters) was appointed consultant project manager and was on-site troubleshooter three days a week for 75 weeks. He didn't have a good impression of the place before he arrived. Old prejudices die hard!

'I always had a pretty unsavoury image of the Tyneside – I used to think it was a dirty mac cinema, or at least screened films that wouldn't appeal to me, but when I first came through the door, I just felt at ease, especially when I met Mark Dobson. I became very enthusiastic about the job. It felt full of hidden secrets – the mosaics and tiles and that. It also had a strong feeling of the heritage of the North East.'

Not that Jimmy – or Mark Dobson and Geoff Cook – had it exactly easy. The combination of listed building and city centre site made work difficult for the builders, Wates. 'Problems just kept on coming. A project such as this is like buying a house – surveys can't show everything. We discovered the stairwell had no proper masonry supports, which slowed us down, but the worst moment was an injunction from a neighbour, which was nerve-shredding till we got it sorted.

'At the end of the day I used to walk from my office at the bottom of Pilgrim Street across the bridge to Gateshead Old Town Hall to brief Mark and I'd pass the big Samaritans sign – 'In Despair? Ring so-and-so...' I often felt like it but I must say Mark never wavered. I'll never forget him saying, we want the same cinema but better.'

Trustee and now chair Simon Elliott came to see the building work not long after it began and remembers how 'heartbreaking' it was to see the torn cinema screen and a hollowed-out building. 'It was distressing but we all had great faith that something special would emerge – eventually!'

Geoff Cook's worst moment during the project was 'seeing one guy digging by himself in the lift-pit with shovel and bucket and thinking, this is going to take forever'. Mark Dobson prefers to remember his high point:

Below and opposite page: Photographer Sally Ann Norman documented the refurbishment of the UK's oldest surviving newsreel cinema in 2008.

'I was leaving the building one night after a long and wearing day and I saw a man at work in the foyer, cleaning the floor in a pool of mucky water. As he swished the cleaner backwards and forwards, the water cleared for a moment and I suddenly saw something gleam – Dixon Scott's translucent tiles!'

Photos © Sally Ann Norman

Finally, on 22 May 2008, the Tyneside was ready for reopening – more or less. Like the original opening in 1937, there were last-minute glitches and delays, but the first audience finally piled through the doors with one eye on the opening movie – Sergei Bodrov's epic *Mongol* – and the other on their new, improved surroundings. I, like many, was entranced.

There were others there that night, watching the watchers, and – after all the hard work and anxiety – enjoying the moment, Geoff Cook among them:

'It was a hair-raising process. We faced potential bankruptcy and went to the wire with various pieces of brinkmanship. It was exciting, flying by the seat of your pants, sometimes spending what we didn't quite have. Mark and I had grown together. He did an amazing job and deserves all the plaudits and the awards the new building has won.'

Among all the happy people that night, there was one with a very particular cause for celebration – project manager Jimmy Floyd:

'I was more engaged than usual. On a job you have to be detached, but this was my baby and I felt I could influence a really special project. It was great to see the place revitalised. There's pride and satisfaction in it.

'But there was something else. My wife came with me that night and as we looked around, she said to me, so this is what you do!

So thanks to the Tyneside for that.'

It is of course fanciful to imagine that, even on such a magical May evening, there might have also been a spectral spectator in the form of the cinema's long-dead founding father, Dixon Scott.

But it does seem slightly spooky, surely, that the triumphant reopening of this, his last cinema, took place exactly 100 years after that of his first, the tiny, ramshackle Kino in downtown Jarrow...

Photos © Sally Ann Norman

The Tyneside Cinema is transformed.

Photos © Allan Mushen & (bottom right) Sally Ann Norman

Roy Pattison

'Where your passions go to enjoy themselves...'

The bare facts of Roy Pattison's life can be set down quickly. He was born in Everton, Liverpool, on 3 December 1948. His mother, as he readily told people, was a 'Jewish Scouse prostitute' who gave him away to a Church of England priest and his wife, who brought him up. He grew up wishing to be a priest himself and in 1971 gained a licence to conduct worship as a lay reader for the parishes of Dunsford and Doddiscombsleigh in Devon. Roy began training for the priesthood, during which time he married and had a daughter. The marriage ended – amicably – as did the idea of becoming a priest. He eventually took a degree in child psychology at London University. In the 1980s he helped set up radical listings magazine *City Limits* and then for the next 20 years helped various arts organisations, including the Tyneside Cinema, through periods of great change, particularly in how they marketed themselves. In the late Eighties he moved to Manchester, where he shared his life with his partner, Tony Russell-Pattison. He died on 10 January 2002, and left a request that no one attend his funeral. His death certificate recorded his occupation as 'Theatre Consultant'. He had ice-blue eyes.

Roy Pattison is the last individual I've chosen to write about in separate biographical panels in this book. I could have written more, but a combination of space and the fact that other individuals who've touched the cinema in various important ways are inconveniently still alive have stayed my hand. I settled on the people I have written about for various reasons: in all cases, it seemed to me they were in their own way remarkable people, with considerable histories and hinterlands, who affected the cinema not merely by what they did, but how they were. It's my personal conviction that an institution as particular as the Tyneside is the sum of the parts of the people who laboured to protect and promote it. Somehow the place has absorbed their spirit.

This is as true of Roy Pattison as anyone. Not that he spent very long in the building – three months in the summer of 2000, and further irregular visits over the following 18 months – but it was a very intense time, for all concerned. Roy would only work on projects in which he passionately believed, regardless of whether they'd be profitable or not. He wanted to be immersed in any commission from the beginning, to be part of the creation of the art.

As he wrote in a letter to his partner, Tony: 'It's not just the end result that is important. I want the process, the journey itself, to be exciting and enjoyable.' His passion for a project could make him manic. According to Tony, he'd work for days (and talk for hours) with no sleep and then at times he'd become depressed and stay in bed for days with Radio 4; these were his 'duvet days'. But at the Tyneside, working alongside Fiona Fitzpatrick and Mark Dobson, there were many happy days, much laughter – and lots of music.

Pattison's musical taste was extremely eclectic, but he had a particular way of listening. For one thing he preferred cassettes, but periodically he'd empty them all and reinsert them randomly into the boxes. In life as in his work, he was fond of playing with the concept of choice. He was, apparently, entranced by the idea of chaos theory when it first emerged.

Despite the fact that in the years they were together, his partner Tony never saw Roy read a book (he thought they narrowed the mind), words were another plaything. That much is clear from the report he wrote for the Tyneside – and the slogan, oddly reminiscent of Dixon Scott, quoted in the previous chapter. It was said of him that he 'dreamed in words and spoke in dreams'. Yet in other ways, he was self-effacing. He always sought a collaborator within the organisation in which he was working (in the case of the Tyneside, Fiona Fitzpatrick); the resulting report was signed with his or her name, to which was added the words, 'And Associates', that happened to be the name of his company. This ensured a sense of equal collaboration, but was useful to Pattison in another way. The anonymous-sounding company was not officially registered: he chose not to join the tax and welfare system and thus kept his existence free from the gaze of the state. For similar reasons he didn't like to have his picture taken.

Tony and Roy were together for 13 years. He writes of their relationship:

'I met Roy in 1989 and loved him. He was like no one I had ever met. I suppose I stalked him a bit, parking outside his flat hoping I could meet him again. Six weeks later I did and moved in the next day. He lived with a man called Dave and we three were together for three years (until Dave moved on). Roy never believed that monogamy was a necessarily good idea. It is impossible to be squeamish about sex when discussing his life. His gradual realisation of his homosexuality led him to passionately embrace the beauty of sex with men. His ideal, he always said was a '19-year-old with beautiful eyes, a PhD and tattoos!' Roy also did not believe in 'casual sex'. Whatever sex might be, it was never casual.

'It could be anonymous, it could be a one-night stand, but it should always be intense, connective and in many instances life-changing. This philosophy extended also to emotional monogamy. Roy believed that you could love more than one person at a time.

'He had a mind the like of which I have never encountered and changed my life and mind for ever.'

The coming of a new century was a difficult time for Roy Pattison: he'd lost two young friends and then Tony was diagnosed with HIV. For years he'd contended with a bi-polar disorder. In his work, he imagined a bold, glittering future for his latest passion, the Tyneside Cinema, but despite the richness of his life, could see no future for himself, and so took his own life.

The priest at his funeral, at Roy's request, read the words from *Compline*, the traditional prayer for the end of the day:

'Be present, o merciful God, and protect us through the silent hours of this night, so that we who are wearied by the changes and chances of this fleeting world, may repose upon thy eternal changelessness; through Jesus Christ our Lord.'

Roy Pattison believed he had no family other than the many intimate friends he took into his life, but two years after his death, Tony Russell-Pattison was contacted by a woman called Rosie, via a private social work tracing agency. Rosie had been adopted and was searching for her birth family. It turned out that she was Roy's birth-sister. Various intriguing details of his family history emerged. His mother's name was O'Neill, which might have meant he was a gentile after all. Despite the trade she eventually took, she went to stage school and learned to dance.What's more, her parents, contemporaries of George Formby and Gracie Fields, toured Britain's variety circuit with an accordion act – they both played, and she danced. In fact her real name was Ada, but husband and wife actually called themselves Eddie and Edie...

Opposite page: Publicity-shy Roy Pattison avoids the attention of a photographer.

Photo © Keith Pattison

It's probably fanciful, but certainly possible, that they might therefore have appeared at the Comedy, the music hall in North Shields that Dixon Scott ran after the First World War, thereby establishing a link between the mogul who built the Tyneside in the 20th century and the 'marketing consultant' who helped reinvent it at the beginning of the 21st.

As a lover of the serendipitous, Roy Pattison would have liked that.

PERIODICALS
SUPPLIED

" The Newcastle Journal "
" The Daily Sketch "
" The Weekly Sketch
" The Northern Echo "
- " The Daily Express "
" The Humourist "
" The Catholic Herald "
" The Geographical
                    Magazine

AND IN THE TYNE ROOM

" The Newcastle Journal "
" The Hexham Courant "
" The Countryman "
" Punch "
" The Landmark "
" Manchester Guardian "

ALSO IN THE SMOKE ROOM

- " The Newcastle Journal "
" The Northern Echo "
" The Times "
The Daily Telegraph and
            Morning Post
" The Navy "
" The Chamber of Commerce
            Journal
" Reader's Digest "
- - " Blackwoods "

TAKE THE LIFT
IN
THE NEWE HOUSE ENTRANCE
BETWEEN THE SILK SHOP AND THE NORTHERN
GOLDSMITHS

ON THE FLOOR ABOVE THERE IS A
LECTURE THEATRE
SEATING 228
AVAILABLE FOR MEETINGS
with
16 M/M CINEMATOGRAPH APPARATUS
SLIDE LANTERN   GRAND PIANO
EPIDIASCOPE
A.C. & D.C. MAINS
WATER AND GAS FOR CHEMICAL EXPERIMENTS.
For Bookings apply to the News Theatre Manager

THE NEWS THEATRE COFFEE ROOM

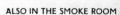

BEVERAGES.

Coffee, Pumphreys Blend including the finest
  Costa Rica and Kenya
    Black or White   per cup   4d
                            per pot   5d
China Tea
  Pumphrey s Blend of Keemun and Ching Wo 5d
Russian Tea with Lemon   5d
Indian Tea, Pumphrey s Tudor Blend   4d
Chocolate   6d
Milk, per glass hot or cold   4d
Horlick s, Milk, 4d   made with milk   6d
Bovril, per cup   4d

SOUPS, various   4d

DRINKS

Lemonade   4d
Grapefruit   4d
Soda & Milk per glass   4d
Fresh Orange Squash 6d   with Soda   8d
Lemon Squash,   4d   "   5d
Orange Squash,   4d   "   5d
Lemon & Barley Water 4d   "   5d
Ginger Beer   4d
Drinks with ices   extra 2d
Schweppes Tonic & Lemon   4d
Whiteway s Cydrax   4d
Iced Coca-Cola   4d

SPECIALITIES.
ICES.

Strawberry Vanilla or Chocolate   4d

FRESH FRUIT SALAD   **8d**
FRUIT (VARIOUS)   **6d**
BANANAS   **6d**
ICE & FRUIT   **6d & 8d**

FOOD

Sandringham Sausage   10d
Tongue   1/2
Hot Dropped Scone (Buttered) (5 mins)   1½d
Hot Girdle Scone   "   "   1½d
Bread & Butter, White or Brown   2½d
Toasted Tea Cake, Crumpet or Muffin   3d
Cakes & Pastries Assorted each   3d
Cut Cake, Cherry   **4d**
        Ginger, Rice, Sultana   **3d**

Preserves
      Grape Fruit and Plain Marmalade
      Strawberry   Lemon Curd
      Raspberry   Pineapple
      Honey   Apricot
      Blackcurrant   ..   .   3d

Biscuits per portion   2d
Chocolate Biscuits, each   2d
Boiled Egg & Bread & Butter   7d
Poached Eggs on Toast   8d & 1/4
Veal & Ham Pies, hot or cold   each 8d
STEAK & KIDNEY PIES   **6d**
CORNISH PASTIES   **4d**

VIENNA ROLL OR BREAD SANDWICHES

Ox Tongue   Cucumber
Banana   Egg & Tomato
Sandwich Spread   Egg & Cress
Tomato   Cheese   Cheshire
                          or Cheddar   each 4d
Crab
Sardine   ..
Salad   each 6d

CHEESE.
With Biscuits, Bread, Plain or Vienna Roll
      Butter Lettuce, Celery, etc
      Cheshire, Cheddar   6d

RATIONING
For some time " The Coffee Room " has been rationed for butter and future supplies may sometimes be limited
Butter will always be served whenever available, but to overcome any shortage we have produced a mixture of butter
and margarine, which will provide a pleasant and nutritious alternative.

The Coffee Rooms

'She stopped, looked around and burst into tears...'

The song was written by Sammy Cahn and Jimmy Van Heusen and sung, unforgettably, by Frank Sinatra in a 1955 musical version of the Thornton Wilder play, *Our Town*. Its instantly catchy and memorable refrain – 'Love and marriage, love and marriage, they go together like a horse and carriage' – isn't simply a sweet reflection of the mores of the time, but also of the symbiotic relationship between the Tyneside Cinema and its equally-revered tenant of the second floor, the Coffee Rooms. As the last line of the song proclaims, 'You can't have one, you can't have none, you can't have one without the other!'

For almost 75 years, give or take the odd interruption, cinema and café have supported each other. Each has its own discrete audience – people who use one institution but not the other – but crucially share a growing number of people who use both. But to me this mutual support isn't just financial: cinema and café share a quirky personality and ethos that relates both to their shared location and birth.

Before we leave that song, one more resonance should be pointed out: over the years countless relationships have been quietly nurtured in the cosy fug of the Coffee Rooms, over a plate of kidneys and gravy, poached eggs on toast, a glass of Cydrax or a cup of plain old tea. Indeed, to my certain knowledge, at least one proposal of marriage was made over a formica-topped table and fittingly, like the end of a Hollywood movie, the couple concerned have lived happily ever after.

Originally, as I've already pointed out, the Coffee Rooms were not meant to be. Dixon Scott Senior wanted to let the space as a tailor's workshop or offices, but no one would stump up the rent of £150 a year. It was apparently the idea of his wife, Virgi, to open a café instead. It was an instant hit and remained so, more or less, up to the late Seventies. For the whole of this 40-year period, the queens of the Coffee Rooms were Virgi and her equally elegant daughter-in-law, Biddy. While their husbands, father and son Dixon Senior and Dixon Junior, ran the cinema operation, they were largely left alone with the catering business.

Opposite page: Wondrous comestibles on offer at the Coffee Rooms, late 1940s.

From the start, the Coffee Rooms were a cut above the opposition: the prices were higher (in 1937, tea and soup were four pence and steak and kidney pie six pence) and the milieu and no doubt the clientele classier. The walls of the main café were decorated with a mural by local artist Bessie Carr of Chaucer's *Canterbury Tales*, and a range of newspapers and magazines was available for – that very evocative word – 'patrons'.

Stop by the entrance to the café today and you'll see a framed menu from the late 1940s. It's impossible not to be struck by the sophistication of what's on offer: drinks include Costa Rican and Kenyan coffees from local importers Pumphrey's; 'Blend of Keemun and Ching Wo Tea (5d), Russian Tea with lemon'; lemon and barley water and Whiteway's Cydrax. Even under rationing, crab and sardine sandwiches are available, along with tongue, something called Sandringham Sausage and the ever-popular poached eggs on toast. Customer are advised: 'Butter will always be served whenever available, but to overcome any shortage we have produced a mixture of butter and margarine, which will provide a pleasant and nutritious alternative.' In spite of rationing problems, *nine* different preserves are offered.

Such superior fare attracted a clientele that was, in the class-infused language of the time, 'a cut above', or at least thought it was. Jean Murray was a regular at the cinema on Friday afternoons in the post-war years, but had coffee and cakes in Woolworth's up the road. The Coffee Rooms evidently weren't for her, or her wage as a secretary at British Paints, not at least until she was married and had more money and perhaps the social aspiration to match. In the 1950s, Ossie Nicholson, a salesman for the Prudential in Gateshead, regularly met his colleagues in the café, where they'd gossip and compare recent commissions. They of course were white-collar workers – wearers of suits and trilbies – and so were staff from the headquarters of the Northern Electricity Board across the road. Kathleen Lumley of Winlaton particularly remembers the girls from NEEB who regularly met in the café, all 'dressed to the nines'.

There's some evidence that blue-collar lads were not so welcome. The Coffee Rooms in those days were policed by their morning-suited manager, the saturnine Mr Hall, who'd been Dixon Scott Junior's batman during the Second World War. He had a little office just inside the Coffee Rooms on the left, a cubby-hole from which he kept a beady eye on his fiefdom, in particular the frequent queues that wound down the stairs. Woe betide anyone who messed about – they'd be sent packing, along with any members of staff from, as it were, below stairs. Clerks were made welcome, but not projectionists, cleaners or maintenance men, even on their days off.

In time, this social protocol began to wither, especially after Mr Hall retired and the benign Biddy Scott took over. She was more tolerant, in all sorts of ways, as her daughter Phillipa remembers: she didn't exactly run a tight ship and some staff allegedly took liberties. As the first director of the Tyneside Cinema, Nina Hibbin offered a different kind of challenge: tough East End communist against genteel Northumbrian 'Grace Kelly'. It was no contest – and in 1978 the Coffee Rooms closed, replaced by a more utilitarian café and seminar room, under the cinema's direct control. It didn't last – and finally the Coffee Rooms reopened and were leased in 1984 to a young caterer called John Oswell, who's been there ever since:

'Back then it was only open between ten and four and very neglected. The water and electrical systems were so antiquated, you couldn't turn everything on at once because the circuit would fuse. For the same reason I couldn't have a cappuccino machine. My parents said I'd never get people to come up two flights of stairs to a café. There was a big risk – I knew that if the cinema died, my business would go with it. But there was just something about it – I had to do it.'

John immediately strengthened the relationship with the cinema, even though director Peter Packer bumped up the rent. He was sympathetic to its history and traditions and saw potential in both longer hours and a shared vision for the future. The founding staff included his brother Jeff (still there), his mam and dad and sister, who worked for free (his mother still does the odd shift) and three sisters called Joanne, Becky and Sue.

'Joanne especially had a great knack of selling. If people asked for coffee, she'd say, would you like milk or c-r-e-a-m? The way she stretched out that word was marvellous – people just couldn't resist it.'

In the 27 years since taking over the Coffee Rooms, John has largely stuck to a traditional menu, tweaking only at the edges, introducing vegetarian options for instance. It's hard to describe the character of the menu, but I'll try: fashionable retro. This seems to fit the broad demographic that is the foundation of the café's enduring success:

'We have every class and age in here. Everyone seems to feel comfortable here – OAPs, students, business people, mums with kids, older women on their own. It's been interesting to watch how kids who came in here with their mams when they were little, they grow up, go to uni and come back and the cycle starts again. And they like to eat what they had when they were young, which also happens to be what the older people like – fish and chips and the like.'

John laughs. 'I tell you, there'd be a riot if we took poached eggs off the menu! A while back, one of my staff suggested we should put egg and chips on the menu, and I pooh-poohed it – no way! But she kept on, saying it would work, and eventually we started with it and it's been a big hit. I suppose it's comforting, as well as tasty.' As an example of which, I offer my nephew, Grahame Chaplin, and his Coffee Rooms' staple. A senior civil servant who travels around the country a good deal, whenever he has a business meeting in the city centre he schedules it in the café and often indulges himself with a 'incomparable' plate of baked beans on toast. Coffee Rooms business meetings take a variety of forms. In the 1990s, actors' agent Janet Plater rented a 'large cupboard' in the cinema that was too small to receive guests, so she regularly met producers and directors in the café, and even held casting sessions with them, with her actors going through their paces in public. Like her, every customer seems to appreciate the personal service.

'We've considered self-service, but I think people love the personal attention – we're not Pret or Costa, we're the Coffee Rooms,' says John.

But this cosy world was threatened when the Tyneside closed for its recent redevelopment in 2006 and the cinema moved to its temporary home in Gateshead Town Hall. John Oswell could easily have given up the business at that stage. Despite the cinema and Gateshead Council wanting the café to make the move too, it was bound to be a big drain on resources. In the end, he took the plunge.

'I was desperate not to make people redundant, my brother included. I didn't want to let Mark Dobson down either – he'd been great to work with and had shown such vision in making the redevelopment happen. It seemed to me there was no café without the cinema and vice versa. But on top of that, there was just something inside. I couldn't walk away.'

Coming back had its problems too. John had to find new carpets, furniture and fittings, but at the same time give the impression nothing had changed. There was almost an endless search for the right dining chair, which caused John sleepless nights. At last the place was ready, with those familiar touches – the old clocks, the James Dean and *Richard III* posters, and the 'For Future Presentation' board, which has been there for years, but ironically came from another cinema altogether. John Oswell waited anxiously for his first customers to return to their old haunts. There was an instant reward.

Opposite page: Monumental public screening of 'Dirty Dancing' in Grey Street, Sunday 4 May 2008.

Photo © Graeme Peacock

'Just as we reopened, one of our regulars came in for the first time. She stopped, looked around and burst into tears.'

9 | 'A History of the Future'

Since it reopened in May 2008, the Tyneside Cinema has enjoyed a period of unprecedented success. This is a statement of fact, borne out by hard, unsentimental statistics.

In 2005-06, its last full year of trading prior to redevelopment, 90,000 people bought tickets. In the first year after reopening – and it was a short year – the cinema attracted 115,000 customers. In the next year – 2009-10, that figure rose to 141,000, producing box-office income of £752,000, which is slightly more than double the figure for the best year prior to the refurbishment. At the time of writing, 2010-11, the cinema is to the end of February outperforming the previous (and so far best ever year) by more than 17 per cent at the box office. The cinema's business plan had set the ambitious target of increasing its audience by a third in the new building. In fact it has risen by more than 60 per cent.

The revitalised popularity of the cinema since re-opening has seen Friends' membership almost triple; bar and concession income rise from £32,000 in 2005-06 to £209,000 in 2009-10; and special project work with young people, despite the harsh economic climate, realise £260,000 in the same year.

Below: The Tyneside Cinema is officially reopened by The Earl of Wessex, 29 January 2009.

Bottom: Sir Ridley Scott, celebrated filmmaker and great nephew of Dixon, speaking on film from Los Angeles to the VIP audience at the first night of the new Tyneside Cinema, 22 May 2008.

More than 400,000 people a year are now visiting a small cinema tucked down a back lane in central Newcastle. As a result, the Tyneside is now making a small profit. In other words, the enlarged and renovated building is delivering exactly – actually, rather more – than what was hoped for before redevelopment.

In this it's been greatly helped by the ever-increasing volume and range of the films it shows. In 1976, the last reopening after temporary closure, the Tyneside Cinema only operated one screen, and didn't have enough new films in the art-house category to fill it. Indeed, looking at the programme for that first year, my impression is that about half the screenings were revivals of classics, or at least films more than ten years old. By comparison, in 2009, of 317 films screened, only 67 were more than ten years old. That leaves exactly 250 *new* films, more or less five a week: a rich programme indeed.

Then there's the range of films. The term 'art-house' has gone, and the Tyneside screens what's now called 'specialised film', a term introduced by the UK Film Council. Such films are often characterised by what they're not: not Hollywood; focusing not on action and spectacle but more on script and character; not conventional, not easily fitting into genres or types. Specialised films often challenge their audience in unexpected ways and inform and educate as well as entertain them.

But the Tyneside, with its extra screen, now regularly shows movies that can also be found at the local multiplex, like the Harry Potter films and *Sex and the City 2*.

Programme manager Jonny Tull is unapologetic: 'Naturally we were a bit nervous about how the established audience might view these mainstream films, but actually the grumbles have been very few. The point about *Sex and the City* is that it attracted a new audience to the cinema. Many of the people who came to see it had never been here before but loved the experience. A lot of them came back for a French film the next week – *Heartbreaker* – and that would never have happened otherwise.'

In fact, before it reopened, the Tyneside carried out audience research, particularly with those crucial 30-40-year-olds who loved film but weren't then actually part of its audience, though they might and indeed should be. The reason they gave for not coming to the cinema was – that old lingering feeling – that it wasn't for them, but for 'weird people'. When they were shown plans for the new cinema, they became very enthusiastic: 'When does it open?'

'The final question from the researchers was the cleverest,' says Mark Dobson. 'They asked what else the Tyneside should do to help them cross the threshold. The answer was that we should occasionally programme something their less film-mad partners would want to come and see.'

That other resonant phrase that dances down the decades:
Come and See...

In all of this, it seems to me, the Tyneside is half-leading and half-following its audience. In the 2010s it could be argued that a typical punter, if there is such a thing, might have a broader taste in movies than his or her predecessor of 40 years ago. As an example, I'd have the same desire to see the re-release of *Back to the Future* as the next Michael Haneke headbanger, and I'd prefer to watch both in the pleasing ambience of the Tyneside, rather than the nearest multiplex. Back in the Seventies, Nina Hibbin understood this, as do Mark Dobson and his team 40 years later.

You don't of course have to take my word for it. Listen to the messages of customers who follow the cinema on Twitter and Facebook:

i wish i could live in the roxy, that would be awesomeeee.
Leyla Richardson, 11 March 2010, Facebook

I've been visiting the Tyneside Cinema for decades. The atmosphere is always conducive to a great night. I have fond memories of a late night viewing of 'Blade Runner' with its first dolby track. And watching 'The Two Jakes' when there was just three of us in the room – me, my friend, and the lady collecting the tickets. I use the cafe regularly – superb, friendly staff. I'd recommend it to anybody. Down with the multiplexes! Real film fans want the personal touch. All the best!
Jeff Myers, 26 August 2010, Facebook

Visited the cinema for the first time at the weekend (originally from Middlesbrough, now living in Ipswich). Awesome, beguiling and beautiful place.
Valerie Peacock, 5 July 2010, Facebook

still can't believe you've agreed to a screening for 30 5 year olds –
very excited :o) x
Lisajane Clark, 24 February 2010, Facebook

I've been to a fair number of indie cinemas in my time, and I completely agree with the Guardian's assessment. Tyneside is easily Number One!
Jonathan David Lim, 22 January 2010, Facebook

We love you Tyneside! :) X
Umbereen Rafiq, 23 January 2010, Facebook

Taking girlfriend to Tyneside Cinema tomorrow. Can't believe she's never been before – she's in for a treat! My favourite cinema.
GrandpaTRex, September 2010

enjoy film in exquisite surroundings where your fellow movie goers seem more like friends than an amorphous rabble
@Haushinkaholic, October 2010

It's a haven & a sanctuary!
@tentspitch, October 2010

I am now far away but the Tyneside is where my mam took us for a lunch as a treat (60s) I saw arty films (70s) I ate a lot of prawn salad when I was pregnant (85) GLAD TO SEE IT SURVIVING 2010!
Denise Rhodes, 23 February 2010, Facebook

love this gem of a place
Agnes R Nicholson, 5 August 2009, Facebook

I'm so glad the Tyneside is open again! I have missed it so much and have so many fond memories which I'm glad to say have not been destroyed by the tasteful refurb!
Craig Daniel Howett, 27 May 2008, Facebook

I don't know how else to put this, so I'm just going to come out with it: I love you. Now let's never speak of it again.
@coconutqueen, August 2010

The prolific British director Michael Winterbottom knows what he wants from a cinema in the 2010s – and perhaps he's not merely speaking for himself:

'As a cinema-goer I want to have the widest choice of films to go and see: whether they're from America or Europe or Hong Kong or India or China or even, God forbid, Britain. But I want to go and see them in a cinema which is designed for them, a cinema which is sophisticated and friendly, a cinema with good projection and sound, which has enough screens to give me a choice of films and which is near the bars or restaurants I might want to go to afterwards.'

He might have been talking about the Tyneside, which is all of these things and more, as another British director noted after a visit in March 2011. Forty years after screening rushes for *Get Carter* at the Tyneside, Mike Hodges returned to Newcastle for a memorable retrospective celebration of his movies. He later wrote the following about the cinema of which he's now a patron:

'I've never been to a better run cinema anywhere in the world. It exudes comfort, warmth, cheerfulness, great programming, good food and drink, everything any cinephile can want.'

But nothing is a given – like everything else in the 21st century, the cinematic status quo can quickly change. The next generation may simply not feel the same way about the Tyneside.

This is one of the reasons why the cinema lays such emphasis on collaborations with festivals and its own special projects programme. The AV Festival, developed from the Light Surgeons project nurtured by Fiona Fitzpatrick and Roy Pattison in 2002, has become the UK's largest international festival of electronic arts.

The second festival to launch at the cinema, in 2003, was the Northern Lights Film Festival, the initial brainchild of Patrick Collerton, which has focused on programming the most exciting new films from across Northern Europe and giving audiences opportunities to meet the filmmakers and encouraging new talent to make films. Finally, as an example of a special project that's taken flight, the festival in 2005 launched the Northern Stars Young Filmmakers' Academy, to provide young filmmakers with a unique year-round training opportunity. This is growing in scope and ambition.

Most people from that generation, Mark Dobson is deeply aware, watch movies not in the cinema, but at home on TV, computers or even phones.

'It's essential we keep up with change, but we'd prefer to lead it. The pace of technological development is immense, but I do believe in the eternal value of the shared experience of places like this. It may be a cliché, but there's something about sitting in the dark with strangers and watching a story unfold that can't be found elsewhere. At heart that's why I feel confident about the future.'

In view of future technological innovation and the likely social change that's equally difficult to quantify, it's hazardous to guess exactly what the future of the Tyneside Cinema will hold, or indeed what a future historian will find to write about it. Much easier then to speak of the past – and the effect this remarkable institution has had on the many thousands of people who've come into contact with it.

As programme manager Jonny Tull puts it: 'It's been a love affair for me, that gets deeper with every year. There've been bad times, and I get really upset when things don't work, but overall they have – and we've got our fun back, like when we had the free screening of *Moulin Rouge* in Leazes Park and 2,500 people turned up. It's been a huge journey, but there's more to come! 'I've the fondest memories of the place – it kept me going personally at one stage, when I split up with my partner,' says Fiona Fitzpatrick, who worked at the cinema for ten years. 'It was my home from home – and the people here were my other family. I used to bring my daughter Millie when she was small and we'd order our teas from the Coffee Rooms and go into the projection box to eat them. She kind of grew up here, she loves films – the next generation!'

But let's leave the very last word to the cinema's longest-serving employee, the occasionally sardonic projectionist Ray Reed, whose 45-year career at the Tyneside Cinema spans the censoring of newsreels with Dixon Scott Junior in the mid Sixties to the screening of films via laptop and digital projector in 2010. His, typically, is not a bad exit line:

'I grumble a bit, most projectionists do, but I wouldn't have missed it for the world. What can I say? It's a building of character that's been the place of some great characters.'

Longstanding Tyneside staff members proclaim their (then) favourite movies. Clockwise from top left: Ray Reed, projectionist and matchless quote-giver ('Das Boot'), former projects manager Fiona Fitzpatrick ('Once Upon a Time in America'), and programme manager Jonny Tull ('The Royal Tenenbaums').

Photos © Keith Pattison

Acknowledgments

First, my thanks must go to Mark Dobson, chief executive of the Tyneside Cinema, and Claire Malcolm, director of New Writing North, who commissioned this book, encouraged its writer and gave unstinting help and advice during its gestation.

Similar warm thanks go to the entire staff of the cinema, but especially to:
Louise Bennett, hires and events officer
Alison Hayes, front of house assistant
Martin Horrocks, finance manager
Rebecca Innes, box office manager
Holli McGuire, projects manager
Samantha Simpson, house manager
Mike Tait, young people's projects officer
Jonny Tull, programme manager
Neil Watson, bar manager
Leigh Venus, venue manager

Also to two trustees:
Geoff Cook, chair 1998-2009
Simon Elliott, former vice-chair and chair 2009-present

My warmest thanks to the following interviewees:
Molly Alexander, usherette, 1939-42
Louise Anderson, cinema researcher
Rob Barnes, graphic designer and Tyneside worker, 1980s
Colin and Maureen Birch, members of the People's Theatre
John Bradshaw, chair of trustees, 1975-79
Jonathan Blackie, cinema patron
Fred Brookes, director Tyneside Cinema, 1984-86
Cynthia and Bill Campbell, cinema patrons
Grahame Chaplin, cinema patron
John Charlewood, cinema patron
Rachel Clearfield, daughter of Dixon Scott Junior
Patrick Collerton, cinema patron, co-director of Northern Lights Film Festival
Elaine Cusack, cinema patron
Peter Ferres, trustee, 1970s
Fiona Fitzpatrick, front of house and projects manager, 1998-2008
Jimmy Floyd, consultant project manager
Judith Green, cinema patron and member of Tyneside Filmgoers Group, 1975-76
Sue Gruellich, daughter of Heini and Rommi Przibram
Anthea Guthrie, daughter of Dixon Scott Junior
Charlie Hall, cinema patron
Rosie Hammond, sister of Roy Pattison
Briony Hanson, director Tyneside Cinema, 1994-95
Lee Hall, cinema patron
Sally Hibbin, daughter of Nina Hibbin
Chris Hurt, trustee and chair, 1976-1996
Maggi Hurt, information officer Tyneside Cinema – and much else, 1979-85
Marjorie and Frank Knaggs, cinema patrons
Jack Kennedy, cinema patron
Jean Murray, cinema patron
Ossie Nicholson, cinema patron
John Oswell, proprietor of the Coffee Rooms
Peter Packer, director Tyneside Cinema, 1986-92

Phil Penfold, former entertainment editor, *Evening Chronicle*
Charlie Picken, manager Tyneside Film Theatre, 1971-75
Janet Plater, Tyneside Cinema tenant, 1990s
Rommi Przibram, actress and Tyneside Film Society member
Lord Ramsbotham, cinema patron
Ray Reed, projectionist Tyneside Cinema, 1966-
Ali Rhind, cinema patron
Alan Riding, projectionist News Theatre, 1954-59
Max Roberts, cinema patron
Tony Russell-Pattison, partner of Roy Pattison, marketing consultant
Ridley Scott, IT consultant and son of Dixon Scott Junior
Ann Tabak, daughter of Dixon Scott Junior
Phillipa Turnbull, daughter of Dixon Scott Junior
Suzy Varty, trustee 1994-2008
Veronica Waters, cinema patron
Doug Weatherall, football writer and cinema patron
Sheila Whitaker, director Tyneside Cinema, 1979-84
Bridget Whitehead, daughter of Dixon Scott Junior
Cyril Winskell, conservation architect
Howard Wollman, treasurer of Tyneside Filmgoers Group, 1975-76
Mara-Helen Wood, cinema patron

My gratitude to the staff of the following libraries:
BFI Library
City Library, Newcastle upon Tyne
The Literary & Philosophical Society, Newcastle upon Tyne

I acknowledge the use of information from the following books:
A Family Named Scott, by Bob Scott (unpublished)
Mass Observation and Histories of Women, by Claire Langhamer
Wartime, Britain 1939-45, by Juliet Gardiner (Headline)
Ryder and Yates, by Rutter Carroll (RIBA Publishing)
Cinemas of Newcastle, by Frank Manders (Newcastle City Libraries)
Cinemas in Britain, by Richard Gray (Lund Humphries)

Photography used in this book is courtesy of:
British Film Institute
British Universities Film & Video Council
Molly Alexander
Steve Lomas (www.lomasphotographic.co.uk)
Photo Mayo
Allan Mushen
Sally Ann Norman (www.sallyannnorman.com)
Keith Pattison (www.keithpattison.com)
Graeme Peacock (www.graeme-peacock.com)
Charlie Picken
RWDP Limited (www.rwdp.co.uk)
Helena Seget (www.helenaseget.com)
David Williams
Jolyon Yates (www.jolyonyates.com)

Finally, my love and thanks to Susan Chaplin, the person who has sat next to me at the Tyneside Cinema for the last 42 years.

Your Tyneside Cinema…

Many reading this book will have memories of their own – in my experience, everyone has a Tyneside story. Please use this blank page to personalise this history by writing down yours. You might also email the cinema with them: more material for the next historian!